Art Of Relationship:
The New Perspective

Ron and Denny Reynolds

TRAFFORD

• Canada • UK • Ireland • USA •

Note for Librarians: A cataloguing record for this book is available from Library and Archives Canada at www.collectionscanada.ca/amicus/index-e.html
ISBN 1-4120-8318-4

Printed on paper with minimum 30% recycled fibre. Trafford's print shop runs on "green energy" from solar, wind and other environmentally-friendly power sources.

Offices in Canada, USA, Ireland and UK
This book was published *on-demand* in cooperation with Trafford Publishing. On-demand publishing is a unique process and service of making a book available for retail sale to the public taking advantage of on-demand manufacturing and Internet marketing. On-demand publishing includes promotions, retail sales, manufacturing, order fulfilment, accounting and collecting royalties on behalf of the author.

Book sales for North America and international:
Trafford Publishing, 6E–2333 Government St.,
Victoria, BC v8t 4p4 CANADA
phone 250 383 6864 (toll-free 1 888 232 4444)
fax 250 383 6804; email to orders@trafford.com
Book sales in Europe:
Trafford Publishing (uk) Limited, 9 Park End Street, 2nd Floor
Oxford, UK oxi ihh UNITED KINGDOM
phone 44 (0)1865 722 113 (local rate 0845 230 9601)
facsimile 44 (0)1865 722 868; info.uk@trafford.com
Order online at:
trafford.com/06-0073

10 9 8 7 6 5 4 3

DEDICATION

I dedicate this book to Denny
for allowing me to be who I am and respecting my ideas
and perspectives, not only during the creation of this
book, but throughout our life together.
Ron

And I dedicate this book to Ron.
The fact that our ideas are equally represented in this
work demonstrates that two people can live, love,
and create as equals.
Denny

CONTENTS

INTRODUCTION

by Ron

Relating to another human being is an art. When we began our relationship, Denny and I had few opportunities to receive formal training or the shared wisdom of experts in the field. In the late 1950s and early 1960s we didn't know of any experts on developing and maintaining relationships. Like any art form, skillful development of our natural relationship talents takes time, dedication, and an understanding of the techniques required to do it well. Nowhere in our educational experience had any kind of instruction or mentoring been provided. Consequently, when Denny and I married as teenagers in 1960, it was pretty much up to us to figure out how to play the relationship game and become happy and successful at it.

Our parents were convinced we were too young to be getting married, and that it would never last. Our falling in love had come on the heels of Nat King Cole's big hit "They Tried to Tell Us We're Too Young" and our parents were worried it was true. They also worried that we wouldn't complete college. Denny did. I did not. I was attending College of the Pacific on a scholarship, majoring in speech with an emphasis on broadcasting. Suddenly opportunities came

1

along to work full time in both radio and television, doing in real life what I was training for in college. In fact, I had already been a successful disc jockey all through high school.

Ours was "love at first sight." We fell in love in 1959 on our way to a college speech tournament in Oregon where Denny would participate in debate and I would compete in extemporaneous public speaking. Somewhere on the road between Stockton, California, and McMinnville, Oregon, it happened and we weren't even in the same car. Denny was in the back seat of one car, gazing though the rear window at me as I drove the next car in the caravan. We stared, at a distance, into each other's eyes for miles and by the time we stopped for the evening in Weed, California, at the foot of Mt. Shasta, we had recognized our deep soul connection.

We were married June 26, 1960. Denny stayed in school to get her degree while I joined the Joe Gamble chain of radio stations in Central and Northern California as a disc jockey and program director. I often did two shows a day for his four radio stations. This was during the early days of rock and roll and top forty radio. At the same time I videotaped a series of children's cartoon shows for KOVR, Channel 13 in Sacramento. I was a ventriloquist with my dummy Jimmy. I hosted *Just For Fun, Wonderama,* and *Cartoonland.*

We managed to cultivate a successful relationship in the midst of extremely demanding schedules and huge responsibilities, which grew to include two sons, born in 1962 and 1964. During the course of our years together we've learned a lot about ourselves and each other and we've paid enough attention to our successes and our failures to gain some insights into our natures and, we believe, human nature. All of which has led us to this second book in our series, *The New Perspective*. In this book we continue to explore spiritual principles and tools for transformation. This time we concentrate on how these concepts can be used to shape happy and healthy relationships, forging a lasting bond of trust and respect. The latest research shows that good relationships are not only the key to happiness, but may be the key to longer and healthier lives.

For me, it is a daily challenge to stay conscious. It requires holding the bigger picture and taming the constant chatter of my mind, to make room for the voice of Spirit. In this book we share a number of insights for relating successfully. If any of them appeal to you and you feel they might enhance your relationship, by all means try them out. See how they work for you.

The insights we share and the relationship principles we advocate are not a guarantee that you will never fight again. Hopefully, the ideas in this book will awaken you and enable you to recognize that when you are fighting with your partner, you're reacting unconsciously in an habitual manner that does not serve you or the relationship.

If I had to choose the number one insight that shifted my relationship with Denny, it would be the revelation that my beliefs create my reality. Once I really had that concept in my heart and mind I could begin taking responsibility for every aspect of my life. This leaves no room for being a victim...ever. Suddenly, it's a new world. It's no longer Denny's fault...or anyone else's fault when I'm not happy with the way things are. Suddenly I can no longer believe that the only way things will get better is if she changes—or they change.

Come with us as we guide you through the steps of shifting your perspective to recognize that the events in your life unfold perfectly for the growth of your soul. There is a blessing in every aspect of every relationship you'll ever have...especially the ones that trouble you the most.

INTRODUCTION

by Denny

We have always been in relationship. From the moment we arrive on the planet our first relationship is with our mothers. Everything we do is in relationship to something else. We only know who we are in relationship. Whether the other is a house, a car, a garden, a pet or a person, we are always in relationship. It is an art to create relationships deliberately and harmoniously. You have to balance yourself, your needs, your wants, and your goals with that of the other. In doing so successfully a third reality is created: a relationship. One and one equal three. This third, the relationship, recognizes the sovereignty of the individuals involved. It produces a blending of energies that has a life of its own, bigger and more than each individual. With us, there is Ron and there is Denny, and there is also what our friends call "The Ron and Denny."

When I say relationship is an art form, I mean that relationships are an artistic blending of the energies of two human beings. Just as an artist blends colors on a canvas to create the picture of what he wishes to convey, we as humans do the same thing. We're just not always conscious of the fact that relationships are about energy coming together. When you use relationship as an art form you paint on the canvas of your life. That's a unique way of seeing what it is we do on this planet as we come together. A good relationship builds love and respect and caring. It sets an example and nurtures and nourishes everyone with whom you come in contact, not only your immediate family but your friends as well. Everyone likes to be around two people who have a good time together and who are in a loving relationship.

I've always been a relationship junky. My great partner in this has been Ron. He and I have been together, growing our relationship for over forty-five years. We have used much of our time together as a living laboratory, applying to our relationship the spiritual principles and tools that we discussed in our first book, *The New Perspective: Ten Tools for Self-Transformation.* In doing so we've both learned a great deal about ourselves and about each other. Relationship is about blending...the blending of me and thee. And it's about blending in a new way. The old model for relationship dictated that I sacrifice for you and put you first and then you sacrifice for me and put me first. The old way suggested sacrifice equaled lasting love. Our new model for relationship requires that I take care of me and you take care of you, and then what we have to give we share with each other.

I have been a Marriage and Family Therapist for more than twenty years. I was drawn to Marriage and Family Therapy because MFTs are relationship specialists. We treat the relationship between husband and wife, brother and sister, parent and child, as well as the relationship we each have with ourselves. Clients come to Marriage and Family

Therapists when their relationships get tarnished. It is our job to help them find beauty and love where they think it no longer exists. *Art of Relationship: The New Perspective* reveals ways to find the love and beauty you believe you've lost.

CHAPTER ONE

A Quantum Leap in Understanding

We believe mankind is on the verge of a quantum leap in understanding that will be as monumental as the Copernican Revolution and will have an even greater impact on how we view the world. In the sixteenth century, Nicholas Copernicus changed people's way of looking at the earth and the sun. Prior to Copernicus, it was believed that the earth was the center of the universe and everything revolved around it. Copernicus proposed that the sun was at the center and the earth and all the planets revolve around the sun. His theory was met with skepticism and criticism, even hostility. It took nearly three hundred years before Copernicus' proposal was accepted. The old theory that placed the earth at the center of the universe now seems as laughable as the once popular theory that the earth was flat. Reality shifted when the description of the earth shifted from flat to round. That and the Copernican Revolution were monumental changes in the way physical reality was defined. We believe a third revolution is coming.

Science has not yet reached a conclusion on how to explain consciousness and reality. Quantum physicists offer a new view of reality by proposing that consciousness is primary, that creation happens from the inside out. We are Spirit, having a human experience. Until this view is accepted, the world remains on the verge of a quantum leap in understanding. The two of us, however, prefer to take the leap now rather than later, living our lives from the perspective that we create our reality through our thoughts and beliefs. We view ourselves as artists, our lives as works of art, each experience as part of the masterpiece.

Artists create physical renditions of inner perspectives. They make real their worldview. They move from within themselves, putting their creation out into the world. This is exactly what we all do, but we do it unconsciously. The artist does it deliberately. When you learn to create your relationships with deliberate consciousness you too become an artist with your life as a canvas. You will begin to see how you take your inner beliefs and act them out in the theater of life by projecting them onto those with whom you come in contact. When relationships are viewed as an art form, we begin to see how they flow and blend and separate and blend again to create a design that reflects the inner reality of the artist. Sometimes it's a harmonious dance of love and light; other times it can be a shocking depiction of fear and darkness. When you allow yourself to view relationships from the perspective that everything is a reflection of your inner reality, you receive a gift. You become more aware of the beliefs that lie deep within you.

The way you conduct yourself in a relationship is based on your beliefs about how life works. If you believe you are a physical body and nothing more, and that when you die you're dead, you'll tend to be competitive and battle for who's right and who's wrong. If you only have limited time you must accumulate everything you can before you're dead and gone. However, if your belief is that there is more to life than meets the physical senses, that life is eternal, then the goal changes. Life becomes an experience, a coming together in relationship for the growth of your soul and spirit. Life experiences change when you ask yourself: "Would I rather be right...or happy?"

We invite you to become explorers, fellow travelers on a journey of expanded awareness. Become an observer. See what shape your life and your relationships take when you assume responsibility for being the creator of your experiences.

CHAPTER TWO

The Sacred Relationship

Lest you think this book, written by a couple who has been together for more than forty-five years, relates only to heterosexual, monogamous, sexually intimate relationships traditionally known as marriage, let us state unequivocally that the principles we'll be describing apply to *all* relationships. Because we have not personally experienced divorce and re-marriage, or monogamous same sex relationships, or poly-amorous relationships, we have not written about them. That is not to say that they are not valid. We write from the perspective of a long-term marriage, because that is our experience. The dynamics and basic truths that govern our closest, most intimate relationships govern all relationships. That's because all relationships are a reflection of the sacred relationship: the relationship we have with our Self. What makes the sacred relationship work makes all relationships work. What tarnishes or detracts from the sacred relationship detracts from every relationship. If you lie to your Self you will not have peace of mind. If you lie in any of your relationships there will not be happiness and harmony. Life has taught us this.

In addition to our own spiritual partnership, we have

had a lifetime of working through the intricacies of relating to our parents, offspring, family, extended family, friends, and workplace associates, including same sex couples and opposite sex couples. The principles contained in *Art of Relationship* cover them all. Participating in such diverse relationships, along with our own successful marriage, has enabled us to formulate the concepts for this book.

A healthy relationship is one based on love, trust, and caring. It is non-competitive, non-abusive, and is not based in domination. It seeks to bring out the very best in each other. The old idea of relationship between men and women was evident in the ancient rite of marriage. This so-called sacred institution was founded on the principle of property rights. Since men were the dominant gender on the planet and could not reproduce themselves without the aid of a female, owning a woman for procreation was essential. Because there was no way of knowing who fathered any child, it became important to claim ownership of the woman and the children she produced. Survival depended upon work being done by a number of individuals. Thus, the idea of "family" came into being. If a man owned enough women and their offspring he could provide not only the basic necessities to survive, but could have enough left over to barter and become wealthy and powerful. Women agreed to this arrangement because it provided safety and security for them and their children— one of the fundamental needs of humankind. This model worked very well for eons, until humankind moved beyond survival and new arrangements were needed.

The time has come to move from marriage, based on property rights and male domination, to Spiritual partnership based on personal responsibility and equality. Personal responsibility in a relationship has many elements. It begins by taking responsibility for your physical being, making healthy choices in nutrition, exercise and life style that allow you to be present with another person, free from addictions. When you're not in good physical health your focus is on yourself and how you feel, leaving you with little to give or share. Being comfortable in your body allows you to place your focus outside yourself so that you can truly enjoy and participate with your partner. Being comfortable with your body, its shape and size, allows you to feel good about yourself. It is also important to be in good mental health and to have the ability to look at yourself and your behavior with some objectivity. Mental illness clouds perceptions and makes it difficult to share an inner sense of well-being.

Spiritual partnership is not based on gender. It is the coming together of any two human beings committed to sharing their spiritual journey. The commitment in a Spiritual partnership is to grow in consciousness and to share and nurture that growth.

⊚⁄⊚

The most important relationship you'll have in this life is the relationship with your Self. Contrary to what most of us were taught, it is not selfish to be Self-centered. We were taught that it is wrong, egotistical, and unloving to think of yourself first. But those teaching us were making no distinction between self and Self. To truly appreciate the difference, we need to share our definitions of self and Self. When we use the term *self* we are referring to the human personality or ego self. This part of us is fear-based and looks at life through the lenses of doubt, judgment, and belief in a negative reality. When we use the term *Self* we are referring to our Spirit nature, the Divine aspect, or the Higher Self. This part of us is based in love and sees life through the lenses of cooperation, harmony, and forgiveness. We believe everyone is more than a skin-encapsulated ego. You are more than your body, more than your ego or personality self. We are all manifestations of Spirit, come to earth in human form to choose experiences for the growth of our souls. We can enhance our earthly experience by awakening to our true nature and what we will refer to as Self-Realization.

Self-Realization is understanding who we really are and our relationship to Source, God, Goddess, and All That Is. Self-Realization is the recognition that the mind has two masters: the human ego or personality self and the Spirit Self. Spirit, that part of Self that is connected to Source, knows that the ego exists. Ego, that personality driven part of the human mind, is totally unaware of the existence of Spirit and must be taught. We believe that by becoming conscious of our thoughts, we can deliberately choose which master we put in charge. Humans have free will, so we get to decide which voice will be in charge of our minds. When we are Self-centered we have made the choice to live life from the center of our Self, recognizing our connection to Source. When we have a good relationship with Self we act from a centered point of well-being and we have good relationships with others.

What does it mean to have a good relationship with your Self? *The New Perspective* acknowledges that consciousness is primary. Consciousness comes first, and all life and life experiences spring from consciousness. We are Spirit having a human experience. It means, as a spark of the Divine, life comes through you—it doesn't happen to you. To have a good relationship with your Self you honor your Divinity. It means you stop indulging in negative thinking, thoughts like "I'm not good enough," "I don't have what it takes," and "I don't belong." It means you learn to stop denying your brilliance. You stop hiding your Light. One of the most important messages of this book is the idea that life works as a mirror: the events of your life reflect your inner thoughts and feelings. The mirror of life takes what's "in here" and puts it "out there" for us to see. As you develop a good relationship with yourself and as you learn to love every aspect of yourself you will see an ever-increasing reflection of loveliness.

The relationship with Self is the Sacred Relationship. It accompanies you through this life from the moment of birth to the moment of death. In fact, we believe the Self exists before birth and lives on after the death of the body, eternally. This relationship provides your inner sense of well-being. This inner sense can be enhanced or diminished by your behavior. Loving acts foster it; fear based actions diminish it. When we use this inner sense of well-being as our guide, we make choices that serve our greater good. More important than striving for happiness is learning to cultivate an inner sense of well-being because this feeling stays regardless of what's going on externally. Even in the face of death and grief and deep sorrow there's room for an inner sense of well-being.

So here we are on planet Earth, going about our lives,

constantly making decisions, our minds working overtime, with most of us giving no thought to which master we've put in charge moment to moment. It is important to remember that of the two masters, ego and Spirit, we decide which one rules our mind and for how long. We have the power to send the ego on vacation and put Spirit in charge, but to do so takes awareness. First, you must stay conscious that both Spirit and ego are sharing space in your mind. Second, you must stay awake, pay attention, and recognize when ego has run amuck and is making choices that do not serve you.

How do you distinguish between the voice of the ego and the voice of Spirit? It is the difference between the voice of fear and the voice of love. Your compass in the world will always be your feelings. First comes thought, then come feelings. Feelings will always let you know whether the thought was ego/personality self generated or Spirit/ Higher Self generated. To deny the barometer of your feelings is to get lost. The joy is that we never have to be lost because we're never without our natural guidance system. We're never without our feelings. We can always check in and ask ourselves: how am I feeling about this? If you feel good, your compass is saying you are in harmony with your Source energy. If you're feeling upset or uncomfortable, it's saying you're out of harmony with your Source energy and it's time for a course correction. Once you figure out how you feel, if you decide you want to feel better, you can make another choice. But you won't make another choice until you can experience where you are right now.

Learning to feel your feelings is not always easy. Many of us have been taught that feelings are bad or need to be controlled or overcome. We have been discouraged from feeling, taught to suppress our emotions. This is particularly true for men who were taught from childhood that big boys don't cry. Our culture teaches that being sensitive to feelings is a sign of weakness. Many women have been taught to hide their feelings as a way to keep the peace and avoid conflict. In Denny's psychotherapy practice she treats people daily who have difficulty feeling their feelings because they confuse feelings with thoughts. It surprises them to learn that feelings register in the trunk of the body and they can be found somewhere between the neck and the thighs. Thoughts, on the other hand, only happen in the head. When you're thinking you're probably not feeling. Feelings, like any other alarm system, can come unbidden and unexpectedly. They simply arise within. Once we cultivate our willingness to notice them, we become better at using nature's guidance system.

Feelings can also provide a signal that you need to take action. When you're in a circumstance, say walking to your car after dark, and you feel a tightening in your belly, it can be a signal to become alert to your surroundings. If you're at a party and you feel a tightness in your chest, it may be a signal that the conversation is painful for you and you need to talk to someone else. Learning to focus on your inner feelings is a major step to becoming Self-Centered. When you know how you feel, at any given moment you'll also know what you need to do to live your life from the center of your Self, honoring your connection to the Divine.

Let us share the story of Sabrina. She couldn't tell her feelings from her thoughts. Sabrina had an adult daughter who was addicted to drugs. Denny asked, "How does that make you feel?" Sabrina began to tell a story about the difficulty she experienced with her daughter's acting-out behavior. Denny asked her again, "But how does that make you feel?" Sabrina persisted with her story. Feelings are very simple. They have no story attached to them. When you're caught in the story, you're thinking, not feeling. Denny then directed Sabrina to look within her body to see if anything of an energetic nature was registering. Did she feel a tightness, a ping, an uneasiness, an inner physical sensation when she thought of her daughter's drug use? Sabrina found the feeling in her chest and the tears began.

Here are some examples of random feelings you might have in the course of a day: happy, sad, jealous, afraid, guilty, depressed, anxious, angry, peaceful, excited, and emotionally exhausted. Caution: feelings should not be confused with judgments. Saying we feel "good" or "bad" is a judgment about a feeling. Therefore, that too is a thought. When you find yourself judging, go one step deeper. What is the feeling that you're judging? Feelings are an inner state. Judgments are thoughts that describe those inner states.

All Feelings Are Self-Generated

No one else can make us feel happy, sad, guilty, depressed, ashamed, or joyful. All feelings are self-generated. If this were not true life would be very easy. When your partner is sad or unhappy all you would have to do to shift that reality would be to pour feelings of joy and contentment into them. This is not possible. When was the last time someone made you happy, sad, or depressed? If you think they did, look again. The other can trigger those feelings, but once your button has been pushed, you manufacture the feelings from within.

Guilt, for example, is very tricky. It never feels self-generated. We even use the expression "he laid a guilt trip on me," as though the feeling came from someone else's power. The truth is we decide when to feel guilty, how bad to feel, and when to stop feeling this guilt. We are in charge of our feelings. When it comes to guilt, we become our own judge, jury, and executioner. Guilt is a marvelous defense mechanism. It is a substitute feeling that we can control. We lay it over places where we feel ashamed of ourselves and then we can experience guilt instead of shame. It also keeps us from feeling how badly we've hurt another person. It protects us from our own conscience. Carrying the cross of guilt allows us to feel separate from those we've harmed and we never have to open our hearts to identify with the wound we've caused. Whenever you're feeling guilty it's important to ask yourself, "What feeling am I avoiding?" "What is it I don't want to look at or experience?" Guilt keeps us from opening our hearts and allowing self-forgiveness and compassion to pour forth. It's also important to remember that feeling guilty blinds us to the reality of the situation. We become stuck in ourselves and we can't see the bigger picture.

CHAPTER THREE

Claim, Not Blame

Just as no one else can generate feelings in you, it's not what happens to you that shapes your life. It's what you do with what happens to you. Taking responsibility for being an active creator in your relationship begins with a pledge—a pledge to the Doctrine of Responsibility:

"I create my own reality...therefore, I am not a victim."

As long as your focus is on what happens to you, you stay in victim consciousness. The truth is, your power is derived from taking action to handle the situation. Taking the pledge requires that you leave all victimization behind. Reclaim your power and stop forever pointing the finger of blame in your relationships.

Because you are creating your reality, it's time to stop blaming and claim responsibility for every aspect of your relationships. Blaming is manifested in two ways. We blame somebody else or we blame ourselves. Either way, we become unable to recognize a deeper reality. We remain stuck in judgment and block any chance at insight or self-awareness. We totally miss seeing and understanding what is behind whatever upset we're experiencing.

It is helpful to understand that all of our relationships are reflections of our inner reality. Everything we see "out there" is a symbolic representation of what exists "in here." This inner reality is composed of both our positive and negative thoughts, both our fears and our loving desires. Because our inner reality, the thoughts and beliefs that live in our minds, is a combination of everything we want and everything we don't want, we get both what we want and what we don't want in real life. Positive or negative, our desire thoughts and our fear thoughts are charged with energy and exist at unique vibrational frequencies. According to the natural laws of the universe, vibrational frequencies attract identical vibrational frequencies. Therefore, our outer experience becomes a reflection of the inner reality. Form follows thought. Life is the manifestation of our inner map of thoughts and beliefs.

Ron's Story

When I was growing up, I learned to deflect criticism by looking for someone or something outside myself to be the cause whenever a problem occurred. Computers have a default position they always return to. I discovered that I also have a default position. Without giving it a thought, my default position tends to be: "I didn't cause that." Sometimes it's a little subtler and less obviously defensive, such as: "What the hell caused that?"

An example of how deeply ingrained this belief is in me occurred at work. I was at the end of my news shift on KCBS and was supposed to end my newscast and join the CBS network news at the top of the hour at nine o'clock. At 8:59 p.m. I was to begin reading my closing headlines, letting listeners know the stories that would be coming up in the next hour. A recorded music theme normally plays underneath this reading of the headlines and a clock device automatically starts that news theme at eight seconds past 8:59 p.m. I began reading the headlines, but to my horror there was no music in the background. Number one, I must keep talking. You can't have dead air on the radio. Number two, I had to figure out what had gone wrong and fix it. My mind raced into action and I decided an electronic failure must have occurred and that the automatic clock had failed to start the recorded music. Deciding I could work around that, I read my headlines and ad-libbed for the appropriate amount of time to take me to 9:00 straight up, when I would push the button that turns on the CBS hourly news and my shift would be over. I pushed the button and there was deadly silence. Again my mind raced into action...now not only had the automatic clock failed, the entire CBS radio network had failed to send the nine o'clock news. Then it suddenly dawned on me...it was not 9:00 p.m. it was only 8:59. I had misread the clock by one minute. You'd think the light would dawn instantly. In fact, it took several moments as I thought about how dark the room was, how hard the clock was to read through my bifocal glasses, while looking around to see if anyone else might be available to share in the blame. This time, no matter how hard I tried, I couldn't wiggle out of it. I was responsible for the problem. In hindsight, I am able to see that rather than being a problem, it was one of the biggest gifts of self-awareness I could have received.

Denny's Story

My default position is: "It's my fault; I'm to blame." My victimhood came in the form of martyrdom. I learned to do this to deflect criticism. If I said it was my fault and began to agonize over my mistake, no one could criticize me or hold me accountable. After all, I was already feeling so bad, how could anyone say anything to me? It would only make me feel worse. I learned very well that a good offense is a great defense. This behavior drove those around me crazy. I was too busy beating myself up to allow others to have an impact on me. This came to my attention when I entered psychotherapy.

One day my therapist challenged me to take a close look at my behavior. She insisted that I was not a victim and that some of the things that happened were "not my fault." I left in a huff, claiming that I was a victim and would remain a victim and everything was indeed my fault. When I returned home, I was met by my son, who announced that our house had been burglarized. For the first time, I experienced what it was truly like to be a victim. Try as I might, I could not make the burglary my fault. This time I really was a victim and I didn't like it one bit. As I looked closer at the circumstance I realized that my statement to my therapist that "I am a victim and I'll remain a victim" opened the door that invited an experience of a similar vibrational frequency. When I realized that the burglary happened at the same time I was speaking those fateful words, I could only laugh at myself. Spirit has quite a sense of humor.

In order to see my part I had to drop my habitual way

of thinking and do some honest inquiry. As long as I believed that everything that happened was my fault, I could
not see the larger perspective. When I found myself blaming myself, I learned to ask: "If there's nothing wrong with
me and this isn't my fault, what's really going on here?"
That simple question has opened up a world of insight for
me. If you are stuck with the invisible belief that you're
to blame, try asking this question and removing yourself
from the equation. This simple tool will enable you to find
a new perspective.

☙❧

As we reveal in these stories, Ron's default position was
to look outside himself and blame others, while Denny's
default position was to blame herself. Neither one of us
was claiming responsibility. We were both faultfinding and
assigning blame. These are very typical male/female responses.

Our different styles or default positions provided fer-
tile ground for arguments, but from those arguments have
come new insights and understandings. There couldn't
have been a better match than our extremely complimentary default positions. From such experiences we've learned
the importance of taking claim, not blame—whether it's
blaming others or ourselves.

We're on the big island of Hawaii as we write this portion of our book. Today we took a drive to Volcano Na-
tional Park. On the way out of the park we passed through
a zone where the volcanic eruptions cause fault lines to
form in the earth. They even have to repave the highway
from time to time to patch up cracks and crevices. We saw

a wonderful sign on the roadside. It said, "End Fault Zone." We decided that's what people in relationships need to do: declare an end to the fault zone.

CHAPTER FOUR

Men and Women: How We Relate

It's incredibly important for people in relationships to be able to talk about their feelings. Major disruptions occur when one person wants to share feelings and the other wants to speak logically about the circumstances. Two different languages are being spoken and no communication is occurring. Men are particularly skilled at diverting feelings with logic. For some men, it becomes their default method of handling such discussions. Some men have an incredible ability to take any situation that their partner is attempting to share on an emotional level and turn it into an intellectual dialogue. Men attempt to problem solve while women merely want an emotional connection. Men and women seem to speak two different languages: a male language and a female language. Most of Denny's work with couples requires her to translate between the two languages. We refer to these differences in communication styles as speaking **man-ese** and **woman-ese**.

Man-ese **and** *Woman-ese*: **A Guide**

Men and women not only tend to have two different languages and communication styles, they also have two different ways of experiencing the world. Men generally experience the world in logical sequence. They tend to function by using primarily the left side of their brains. Women, on the other hand, usually are more global, seeing things holistically and feeling things intuitively. The right side of the female brain tends to dominate. While men are the doers, women are the receivers. This is not the case one hundred percent of the time, but in general form follows function. Men are the outies, women are the innies.

Women are raised to have their feelings. It's been okay over the years for the female of the species to feel, even though she may have learned to be careful about openly expressing those feelings. Men, on the contrary, are seldom allowed the full range of their feelings because of the cultural definition of masculinity. When you take inborn, natural characteristics and add cultural conditioning to them, our distinctive styles become even more firmly entrenched. Furthermore, those differences become more pronounced and more challenging in the context of a relationship.

As a Marriage and Family Therapist, Denny's job is to sit with couples and help them understand, respect and appreciate their different styles. She helps men see that there's something deeper going on when they're stuck in their left brain intellectual perspective by directing them to a deeper part of the Self. When women come for therapy, totally immersed in their feelings with no way of talking about it, they need to be directed to their intellect so they can express in words what they're feeling and needing. In a good relationship, you don't have to fight over whose way is the right way. You can simply accept the fact that these are two different ways of experiencing the world. Two different styles, two different ways of being. No one has to give up his or her way. If the man can learn to appreciate the woman's style and the woman can allow for the man's way of being, you can have communication. Each can learn to understand the other, while acknowledging the differences.

There are no hard and fast rules. Nothing is one hundred percent certain. Not all men are "thinkers" and not all women are "feelers." Our descriptions are generalizations. We've known relationships where the woman was the "thinker" and the man was the "feeling" one. Same sex relationships can have interesting combinations of "thinkers" and "feelers" or "thinkers" and "thinkers" or "feelers" and "feelers." What exists in one circumstance may not exist in the next. That's why it's necessary to be sensitive to the flow of relationship. Relationships are not static; they are constantly changing and evolving. That's what makes relating an art form. We stay in relationship flow when we act from our inner sense of well-being.

The Battle You Don't Want to Win

Men and women also have different underlying negative beliefs about themselves. Generally speaking, men are primarily concerned about their productivity. Their self-talk centers around whether or not they're able to produce enough. Can they do a good enough job in the world? Can they be good providers? Women, on the other hand, worry about their attractiveness. Their self-talk centers around the question: am I attractive enough, interesting enough, smart enough to hold my partner's attention? With these underlying negative self-beliefs it becomes very difficult for couples to understand each other. Most women do not doubt the productivity of the man they're with, despite his self-doubt. They have more faith in his ability than he does. Men don't doubt the woman's attractiveness. It's a given that they find her attractive or they wouldn't be in a relationship with her. The problem is, when we're functioning from our own negative beliefs, no one else exists. We're too caught up in ourselves to sense that the other person even has an issue. Most men would be shocked to learn that the woman they've chosen for a partner worries that she's not attractive. Most women can't conceive that their man doubts his ability to produce. In relationship counseling it becomes necessary to unwind those negative beliefs in the presence of each partner. This allows couples to reach a deeper understanding of the person with whom they're involved.

Couples often come to therapy ready to defend their positions. Often the man will be upset with the woman because he thinks she wants too much. What the man doesn't realize is that the woman's appetite is great because she has total faith in his ability to produce and provide. The man, doubting his ability, focuses only on his fear that he'll not be able to afford everything she desires. Women often come to therapy complaining that the man's focus of attention is not on her. These women have a secret fear that something else is more attractive. The women complain that he spends too much time watching football or playing golf. In doing this, the woman believes that his preoccupation with sports is a result of her unattractiveness. She forgets that he's a separate person who like many men, really enjoys sports. The truth is, not only is it not her fault—it's not even about her.

These are arguments that neither party should really want to win. They're both arguing to defend their fears. Both partners are arguing for their limitations. If either one of them wins, that's what they'll be stuck with: their limitations. As a therapist, Denny has found that if the woman wins and convinces the man that she's right, and he then joins her in not believing in her attractiveness, the relationship is in deep trouble. The same is true if the man convinces the woman that he is no longer productive. The relationship has little chance of survival when both partners buy one partner's basic fear, whether that fear is doubting attractiveness or productivity. Take a look and see if you can spot where this dynamic lives in your relationship. Recognition of this dynamic and being willing to own your part and make a course correction can bring your relationship back into loving harmony.

We made the case in our first book for the idea that your beliefs create your reality. Now we're reminding you that life lived from negative beliefs is based in fear and creates a reality you do not prefer. Shifting your perspective to self-acceptance creates a positive reality based in love, joy and happiness. You live in a free will universe and you choose your beliefs moment to moment. Your beliefs today determine your reality tomorrow.

CHAPTER FIVE

Over-giving and Over-taking

Just as men and women have different ways of perceiving the world and communicating, so they also tend to follow different behavior patterns in relationships. One common dynamic is over-giving and over-taking. For example, let's say you're in the midst of making a phone call. This call is important to you and you need to make it now. Your partner interrupts, asking you to sit down and help him go through the incoming mail. If you stop your phone call to please him, you have sacrificed. You may have given, but you have given with a string attached. You now feel he owes you one and the energy string will stay attached until the debt is paid. And if it's not paid when you expect it to be and in the manner you demand, you'll become filled with resentment. This negative undercurrent does not foster a loving relationship. If you add up all the small incidents like this, you'll eventually convince yourself you're living with an insensitive person who thinks only of himself. The truth in this example is that your partner didn't ask you to give up what you were doing. He wasn't even conscious that you were involved in something. He only wanted your involvement with him. It is up to you to communicate your needs and preferences. A simple statement such as, "We can go through the mail together when I'm off the phone," can produce a better outcome. Being honest and honoring your Self-interest nurtures harmony, instead of resentment.

It is very important in establishing and maintaining a close and loving relationship to learn to put your Self first. You have to take impeccably good care of your Self. You have to be Selfish, in the sense that you stay in touch with your own inner sense of well-being at all times. You need to be willing to tussle with your partner if necessary to maintain that inner sense of well-being and not be tempted to sacrifice it. Avoid the common tendency to discount your needs for fear of displeasing your partner.

Another part of over-giving is giving yourself the right to define everyone in your life, thinking you know them better than they know themselves. This is very disrespectful. You may feel entitled to do this because you have been so generous. After all, in your head, you've been plotting and planning what you will do for them to take the very best care of them. You're certain you're right when you're giving these gifts of time, energy, and focus. It's important to note that this is all going on in the head of the over-giver. The other doesn't even exist. The over-giver has not asked what is wanted or needed.

The real damage that occurs with this dynamic is that the over-giver begins to believe that he/she is right and that they see a truth that the other is hiding from them. Consequently, the belief becomes, "I know you better than you know yourself." The reality is you only know the story you tell yourself about the other and you have no idea what is really going on inside them. But when you think you already know, there's no need to ask. You just assume. Ask. Don't assume. Remember, **assume** makes an **ass** out of **u** (you) and **me**.

Denny's Story

As the child of an alcoholic family system, I learned to survive by reading the undercurrents of the family dynamics. These undercurrents are the unexpressed feelings and suppressed emotions that exist in the household. It is a vibratory frequency that creates a wide gap between words and reality. When this happens feelings and truth are not discussed—they're stuffed. Stuffing them does not make them go away. Instead, it creates a negative vibration. While no one may admit it, everyone feels it. The children in the family are very aware of the discrepancy. They search for a way to make sense of what's going on. They learn to tell themselves a story so they can figure out how to be safe. The frightened child gets comfort and reassurance from the story. Since children feel that they are the center of the universe, this story always makes them the cause for whatever issues are not being discussed. Growing up in these circumstances, I learned to make myself the reason for the problem. I believed that in order to make things better all I had to do was change my behavior, and the unspoken bad feelings between my parents would go away. This is how I learned to be an over-giver. As a result of this coping mechanism I spent years trying to change my behavior to make unpleasant situations better. Try as I might, my solution never worked, but I attributed that to my inability to behave properly rather than a flaw in my thinking. I took on everything as though it were my fault.

With this pattern established, I married Ron. For the first seventeen years of our relationship I read undercurrents. I tried to interpret the hidden meaning in every uncomfortable situation. If Ron came home angry, I believed on a deep level I had done something wrong. At those times I would fall into my geisha role. I did everything but rub his feet and I would have done that if I had thought it would help. Because I was so stuck in my belief that it was my fault, I couldn't even ask him what was wrong. If he told me what was troubling him, I didn't believe him. I knew better. It had to be something wrong with me. After seventeen years of over-giving, I developed a bit of resentment. He was ungrateful and insensitive to all I did for him.

One of my favorite solutions was to "shop at him." Whenever I decided he was a total jerk, I would go out and buy anything I wanted. After all, I deserved it. I gave him everything and what was he giving me...nothing. So I had the right to spend as I pleased. It didn't matter that we might not be able to afford it—I was entitled to what I wanted. This worked for as long it worked, but the fight about finances was not pretty. Imagine my surprise when Ron and I ended up in couple's counseling and he began to tell me what he really wanted in a relationship. All that geisha giving was not at the top of his list. Not only had I been over-giving—I'd been giving the wrong things. What a shock that was. In the course of couple's therapy I found myself telling the therapist what Ron was feeling and thinking. The therapist would stop me and say, "Let's ask Ron about that."

His answer was not the same as mine. I was speechless. I began to listen to him. I began to discover who he was and I saw for the first time a being separate from me. I experienced humility when I realized that he knew himself far better than I did. He was the person who lived within his own skin, not me.

In the course of our couple's counseling the therapist challenged us to earn each other's trust and respect. Since Ron had earned my trust, I was forced to believe his words rather than my story. I felt I was awakening from a deep sleep. Suddenly the world around me was peopled with individuals whom I knew nothing about. I became aware that my judgments were more about me than the people I judged. This was a major shift in consciousness for me. Not only did our couple's counseling put us on the course of trust and truth, which helped us through a very rocky time, but it also led to my becoming a psychotherapist.

◎◎

There are always two sides to a situation. In order for relationships to be equal, in the midst of one person over-giving, there must be one partner who is over-taking.

Ron's Story

In the early years of our marriage, I was very caught up in my radio career. As difficult as it is to admit, my job was often more important than my family. I not only had to be a successful disc jockey three to four hours a day, I was often the station program director. This required that I work ten and twelve hour days. Worse yet, I was constantly listening to the radio station on weekends—never taking a trip without the radio on, shushing my wife and kids if they talked while I was trying to listen to the disc jockey. I wasn't present for my family: I was a working program director and talent scout. At the end of many a long day, rather than coming directly home to a harried housewife who was struggling to take care of two young children, I'd stop by the bar to play a little liars' dice with the other disc jockeys. I felt entitled to this less than sterling behavior because I was the bread winner. I rationalized that all that hard work was for the benefit of my family. I conveniently overlooked the fact that I was involved in a fun and exciting career that I had wanted since I was eight.

It took a lot to get my attention off radio and on to anything else. Denny's shopping was about the only thing that got my attention. Then I told myself it was a good thing I worked as hard as I did and made the kind of money I was making. Denny was right; I was insensitive, but not for the reasons that she thought. I was more unconscious than anything else. Couple's counseling was a real eye opener for me as the therapist guided us through the process of truth telling and I began to get a look at Denny's perspective. For the first time, I was forced to take an objective look at myself and my behavior. I could see that Denny was indeed over-giving. But even worse—I was over-taking. I began to see how poorly I budgeted my time, how little I gave Denny and the kids, and how much I relied on her support of my career. I finally began to get in tune with my family—the start of my becoming more sensitive.

Ron's Day of Awakening

We had been married for about ten years when something happened that put me in touch with how much I took Denny for granted. What happened made me realize how much I unconsciously accepted her "over-giving" without stopping to appreciate everything she had done for me. It was one of the rare times Denny and the kids had gone away for the weekend, and I was left to fend for myself. Since I had never learned how to cook, when alone I usually relied on fast food or take-out dinners. But this time I decided to take care of myself with a home-cooked meal. The only cooking I knew how to do was to barbeque, so I stopped by the supermarket and picked out a nice filet mignon, bought some charcoal, came home, prepared the fire and lit the barbeque. I poured myself a nice glass of red wine and proceeded to barbecue my filet to perfection. I really did a great job. All went well until I took the steak off the grill and put it on a plate. Not until then did it dawn on me that was all I had for dinner. The baked potato, asparagus, fresh salad, French bread and other tasty parts of the meal that had always magically appeared every other time I barbequed failed to materialize. I was ashamed and embarrassed by how much I had taken Denny's contributions for granted. I sat down in front of the television with my glass of wine and lonely steak and appreciated Denny more with every bite I took.

☯

As we both woke up and saw what we were doing to each other we began to walk a new path, a spiritual path together. At the direction of our therapist we began to look inside for that inner sense of well-being. We learned to use that as our guide on how to treat each other. Denny learned first hand that sacrifice doesn't work. Ron learned first hand that self-involvement doesn't work. Neither produces a happy and harmonious relationship.

We learned to put our relationship first. We learned to make choices for the sake of the relationship, not for ourselves. We learned to give joyfully and with an open heart. We now make choices that respect the other person and avoid creating strife because we realize how much that would hurt the one we love...and how that in turn would detract from our inner sense of well-being.

CHAPTER SIX

Conflict, Duality, and the Shadow

No matter how much two people love each other, it is inevitable that sometimes they will find themselves in conflict. When this happens, it's important to remember the problem is not with the other person. The problem lies within. Conflicts present an opportunity to look at our shadow sides—the unowned aspects of ourselves. The shadow side is that part of ourselves with which we struggle; the part that's easily angered, jealous of the success of our friends, feels superior to others and will do anything to win. We try to hide these unpopular parts. This is our Shadow.

Recognizing that we have both positive and negative traits, both thoughts of love and fear, it's helpful to understand that we achieve wholeness only when we've learned to love our whole selves. This includes our shadow nature. The term Shadow was originally used by Carl Jung to define the parts of the self that we do not acknowledge. More recently, excellent work has been done by a number of pioneers, devising techniques not only to recognize our Shadows, but to dialogue with these hidden aspects, gaining a greater appreciation of the role they play in our lives. Some of the shadow work we've found effective has been inspired by and evolved from the writings and techniques of Hal and Sidra Stone and Debbie Ford. We're grateful to Hal Stone, Ph.D., and Sidra Stone, Ph.D., for their technique called *Voice Dialogue,* which is an in-depth study of the many selves or sub-personalities that make up the human psyche. The Stones developed *Voice Dialogue* as a method for working directly with these selves. They have written a number of books on the subject, including *Embracing Our Selves, Embracing Each Other,* and *Embracing Your Inner Critic.* We have also found Debbie Ford's work extremely helpful. We recommend her books, which include *The Dark Side of the Light Chasers, The Secret of the Shadow,* and *Embracing Your Dark Side.* In her books she gently guides readers to identify their shadow aspects, while encouraging a new appreciation for the positive contributions of these aspects.

To become conscious we must look at our whole being, even though it is difficult to acknowledge that we are both good and bad, loving and fearful, powerful and weak, happy and sad, light and dark. For some of us, this realization is so painful that we refuse to take responsibility for having these negative aspects. When we have one of these negative feelings we deny our experience and pretend that it's not part of us and that it's coming from outside of us. Sometimes the only way these parts of us become available for examination is when we are in conflict with another person. The conflict puts us in a state of Grace that gives us an opportunity to observe the Shadow in action, and thus the opportunity to experience Divine Conflict. By viewing the conflict from this new perspective, we allow our souls to grow.

The Shadow in Action

Fights are never about what you think they are. What you think you're fighting about usually has to do with a grievance, what you think someone did to you. This is how we experience our Shadow. It feels like the person you're in conflict with is behaving badly and you are his or her victim. What's really happening is that you're interpreting what their behavior means, based on what's going on inside you. You think it's coming from the other person, but it's all happening inside you. If you can go deep enough into your being, you will find that you're the one who is judgmental, mean, jealous, or insensitive. Because these unwelcome expressions don't match the image you have of yourself, you project them outward and see them as coming *at you* rather than *from you*.

Others easily see our shadow side. Generally speaking, we do not. However, the universe has provided an incredible mechanism by which we can see the hidden side of ourselves—the Shadow that lurks within. The mechanism is called projection. It works the same way a projector in a movie theater works. It casts the image, the story, outside of itself onto a screen so it can be seen and fully appreciated by the perceiver. We project our shadow side outside ourselves, so we can see it, and become conscious of it. And we do this all the time. We do it in every relationship. We project dark and light shadow traits outside ourselves onto the people with whom we are in relationship, so we can see the traits that would otherwise be hidden from us.

The two of us laughingly refer to life as being a wonderful and mysterious magic trick. It's a trick—it's done with mirrors. Since we can't see our own shadow side, we must look outside ourselves at our various relationships that mirror back to us our hidden, inner realities. Next, we must become aware of whatever judgment we have about the relationship we're observing. When the voice within says or thinks, "Mary is a wonderful friend, but I wish she weren't so sarcastic," it's time to take a look at our own relationship to sarcasm. We heard a line on the *Oprah* show recently that we've found extremely helpful: "If you can spot it, you've got it." When you see something you don't like in someone else, it is also in you. This is a huge step toward self-realization. We make tremendous strides when we look outside ourselves at each projected trait and then claim it as our own.

By examining the parts that you don't want to acknowledge, you have an opportunity to learn something about yourself. When you can see and integrate the shameful, unbearable, painful, unattractive features you possess, you grow.

To benefit from an argument, we recommend you ask these questions: What does this argument represent? What does it say about me? This exploration of self takes courage, but once you bravely take the step and ask the questions, we guarantee you'll learn something profound about who you are. So ask yourself in a very deep way, "By blaming, what am I not seeing about myself?" Or if you're blaming yourself ask, "What part of the bigger picture am I not seeing?"

The following exercises are designed to help you see the hidden Shadow parts of yourself.

Facing Your Shadow

Pick a difficult relationship that really troubles you. It could be a long term or fairly recent relationship involving a partner, relative, friend, boss, or co-worker. Allow memories of this relationship to come to mind. Write a brief description of a specific incident that made you unhappy with this person. Now answer the following:

How did that person make you feel?

What was your judgment about their behavior?

Have you ever behaved in a similar fashion?

If not, can you imagine a circumstance in which you could behave this way?

What unowned, unloved, or unacceptable aspect of yourself did this process help you discover?

Can you identify this aspect, such as selfishness, stubbornness, or jealousy?

Claiming Your Shadow

As you think about the most difficult person in your life right now, be extremely judgmental. Don't edit yourself or be nice—let it all hang out. Write what you really feel.

Write three words to describe the person you have in mind:

1._____

2._____

3._____

Now, starting with **word number one** write: I am_____ _____ (that trait: stubborn, selfish, or whatever you wrote for number one).

Write this at least ten times.

Next, move on to **word number two** and do the same thing: I am_____ (that trait).

Write this ten times.

Finally, move to **word number three** and write: I am__ _____ (that trait).

Write this ten times.

Take a moment to reflect on how you felt during the exercise. What was the most difficult part? Which word bothered you the most? What trait was the most difficult to own?

Next, write about a time *you* exhibited that trait, or someone else might say you exhibited that trait.

If you can't remember ever exhibiting the trait, imagine under what circumstances you might exhibit that trait.

This is a difficult exercise. It requires a lot of introspection and thought, but it is very revealing. Now, it's time to lighten up. If you were to give a nickname to this Shadow Aspect, what would it be? Write the first thought that comes to your mind: Bitchy Brenda, Stubborn Sam, Asshole Allen, Mean Mike, etc.

Exploring your Shadow side is a process of self-discovery. It's a bit like traveling to a foreign country. You never know what you're going to find until you get there. But each Shadow aspect has something special to offer. The following exercise will allow you to further explore this new territory and receive your Shadow's gifts.

You may want to record this guided visualization and then play it back and experience it, or you may prefer to read it and then silently repeat the experience in your mind. Another highly recommended method is to ask your partner to be your guide through this process. This guided journey is also for sale as a CD on our web site *www.thenewperspective.com*.

Encountering Your Shadow

Close your eyes and take five deep breaths. Imagine standing at the stairs that lead to the basement. Invite your Higher Self to accompany you on this journey into the darkness of the basement. Your Higher Self will always keep you safe and support you on your journeys. Now begin to count as you take each step down the stairs. With each step you're becoming more relaxed, comfortable and confident about your journey. One, two, three...becoming more and more relaxed and secure as you step deeper and deeper into the inner space of the basement. Take as long as you need and as many steps as are necessary to descend all the way to the bottom. As you look around the basement you find two very comfortable chairs where you feel totally safe and relaxed. A figure sits in the shadows in one of the chairs and motions to you to take your place in the other chair—which you do, sitting down comfortably, facing this dark figure in the shadows. As you adjust to the darkness you're able to notice in great detail various aspects of this shadowy figure. Take time to notice as much detail as possible.

Is the figure male or female?

How old is the Shadow?

What is this Shadow figure wearing?

How do you feel about him or her?

Ask for your Shadow's name and listen carefully to the answer.

Now, invite the Shadow to speak the truth to you. Ask it to tell you what its role has been in your life.

What gifts has it brought you? How has your Shadow assisted you in this life?

Now, ask what your Shadow needs from you. Take as much time as you need to listen to what is said.

When you're ready, thank him or her for the help that has been given you. In your own time, when it feels appropriate, leave the basement and journey back up the stairs—each step bringing you back more and more to this room. With each step up the stairs you become more alert, awake, fully remembering everything that happened in the basement and everything that was said by your Shadow. Come back up and be aware of the seat you're sitting in. When you're comfortable, open your eyes.

@/@

It can be extremely helpful to take a moment and write a few paragraphs about your experience. These visualizations fade from memory quite quickly—like a dream, so write in as much detail as you can while it's fresh in your mind. Write what your Shadow looked like, felt like and said. Its name...its role in your life...the gifts it has given you...the assistance it has been in your life. What did your Shadow need from you?

If writing about your experience does not feel comfortable or appropriate at this point, consider drawing a picture of your Shadow self. After you've completed your picture reconsider doing the written exercise.

To summarize what we have learned about our Shadow aspects: they are what we usually consider to be the unpopular, negative ways we behave. However, without both our positive and negative traits we are not complete, which is why it's important to recognize our Shadow sides, embrace the behavior, and explore the possibility that the Shadow may have a gift for us. Things you resist tend to persist, so it's much more healthy to move out of denial and into acceptance and wholeness.

Now that you have recognized one of your Shadow aspects it's time to take the next step.

Own It, Feel It, Release It

STEP ONE
First, take a deep breath. Think back to one of the Shadow aspects you identified in **Claiming Your Shadow.** Recognize that you are seeing a part of yourself. Despite the negative judgment you have, it helps to say, "This too, is me."

STEP TWO
Second, stay with your feeling of judgment until it begins to shift and you experience some inner relief.

STEP THREE
Now ask yourself, "When was the last time I behaved that way and what triggered that behavior?"

Stay with whatever feeling or memory arises. Allow yourself to feel uncomfortable, embarrassed or ashamed. Just stay with it. Don't resist it. Embrace it. If you don't resist, it will move through you.

In this process, **Step One** (Owning It) requires action by you. **Step Two** (Feeling It) is something you allow. **Step Three** (Releasing It) happens by itself. There's nothing you have to do.

The process of **Own It, Feel It, Release It** is something our friend Dr. Sharon Wendt wrote about in *Radiant Heart, Healing the Heart/Healing the Soul.* It will eventually enable you to move beyond judgment as you learn to truly love every aspect of yourself. Self-love is the basic tenet of the *Art of Relationship.* It is only then that you can truly love others, because others will always symbolize and reflect back aspects of yourself.

The shadow self is always an unowned part of ourselves, but it is not always our dark side. We sometimes don't own the good and loving parts either. As we come to recognize our Divinity, our God-Self, they will be reflected back in our life experiences as well.

Failure to own the Shadow keeps us from being whole. We are suggesting that these polarities (good/bad, light/dark) that seem like opposites be conceptualized as dualities. Rather than seeing them as opposites, notice that they both exist as part of the whole. It's similar to a magnet, which has a positive pole and a negative pole, but both poles exist on either end of the same magnet. Thus, the world can be seen as organized according to the principle of duality, rather than opposites: Yin and Yang, day and night, hot and cold, up and down. You can't have one without the other: both are different aspects of the same thing. They are complimentary aspects of the greater whole. Therefore, to be complete we must learn to recognize and embrace both our positive and our negative traits, both our light side and our dark side, both our loving selves and our evil twins.

CHAPTER SEVEN

Arguments

In considering arguments, we need to remember the concept that all situations are fundamentally neutral. The only meaning they have is that which we assign. Taking a look at the meanings you assign during arguments is another way of discovering your Shadow side and revealing your hidden beliefs.

How does an argument happen? Someone does or says something to upset us and we react. As difficult as it may seem, this reaction is based upon what we are feeling and believing, not on the other person's behavior. We assign a negative meaning based upon our fears. And we do it all the time. We perceive through a fear-based filter with a bias. During arguments we *forget* this important principle: all situations are fundamentally neutral.

The Anatomy of an Argument

At the height of a heated discussion Denny reaches over to pull open the drapes and in the process the drapery cord breaks. Ron says, "Look what you did, you broke the drapes."

Denny hears that as "It's your fault. You're careless. You should be more careful." In the meantime, Denny is thinking, "How dare you judge me? How dare you hurt me? How dare you tell me what I should do?"

And Ron is thinking, "The drapes are broken. It's Denny's fault for being so careless."

Ron and Denny find themselves once again in their default positions. Ron is pointing the finger of blame at Denny because somebody, other than him, must be responsible for this problem. Inside, Denny is pointing the finger of blame at herself. On the outside she has become defensive because she's afraid it might be true that she is careless.

One person says something. The other person reacts. The question becomes: what am I reacting to? How am I perceiving this situation, and what am I believing about myself?

The fact of the matter is the drapery cord was 25 years old and had simply worn out. A quick, firm pull of the cord by anyone would have produced the same result. The situation was neutral. It was just something that happened. There was no cause and effect, no good or bad, no right or wrong.

A more enlightened, productive way to look at this situation now enables both Ron and Denny to reset their default positions and recognize the gift...the role the other played in prompting self-examination. As a child, Denny was often criticized by her parents and was told she was careless. She continued as an adult to struggle with that Shadow side of herself. Ron, on the other hand, now recognizes that he tends to rush to judgment and is quick to blame others when problems occur. Ron got to look at a Shadow aspect that had lurked within him since childhood.

By becoming conscious and observant we can decide our old beliefs are not valid or we can decide our old beliefs have a ring of truth that can be the foundation for adjusting or improving the way we behave in the future. Either way, the argument has definitely provided an opportunity for self examination—as all arguments do. Every argument is an opportunity to get to know and love another aspect of yourself.

Caution: the opportunity to grow can be totally aborted if couples allow the argument to escalate beyond control. When you become angry and enraged, it may release your own feelings, but it does nothing to improve the relationship. Dumping anger has to do with making yourself feel better by making yourself feel right. Such action is ego involved and takes away any possibility of getting close.

Anger

There's nothing wrong with being angry and expressing that anger. It's how you express it that counts. If you can learn to speak your anger in a non-explosive way it will benefit the relationship. When anger is used as a weapon to win an argument, it's destructive to the relationship. When anger is expressed in a disrespectful way—when there's name-calling or yelling or accusations—nothing productive is accomplished.

In her practice, Denny has witnessed a recurring dynamic she refers to as "Nice Guy/Bitch" or "Innocent

Damsel/Bastard." The Nice Guy or Innocent Damsel who doesn't easily express anger has learned to transfer that feeling energetically to the partner. The Bitch or Bastard then takes on the anger for both of them. When this anger can no longer be contained, it comes roaring forth. This allows the quiet partner to feign innocence, "See what a nice person I am, I don't know why I'm being treated this way." It's a very destructive game. How often do you play this game in your relationship? This dynamic can be rectified if the Nice Guy or Innocent Damsel becomes aware of their angry feelings and learns to express them in a constructive manner. It can also be rectified if the Bastard or Bitch refuses to take on anger that does not belong to him or her.

Anger is a two-part emotion. First you get your feelings hurt, then you get angry and lash out. If you can learn to say, "Ouch, that hurts," you will shift from ego being in control to speaking from the heart. Learning to speak from your pain and vulnerability slows down the argument. Instead of continuing the argument to the point of anger and resentment, which are both based in fear, you can learn to use love to transform it. During arguments we give up our role as a creator and we default to being a reactor, responding to a negative dynamic. Notice how similar the words are: *creator/reactor*. Reactors respond to something they perceive to be happening to them, or coming at them. Creators know that life flows through them and they take responsibility for manifesting their reality. The only difference between *creator* and *reactor* is the placement of the letter "c." Why not let that "c" stand for *consciousness*? When *consciousness* comes first you create your reality and you no longer react as a victim. The argument is over.

Think back on the last argument you had with your partner. Can you find your default position? Where do you automatically go in times of crisis? What causes you to react?
Can you begin to see the sacredness of your relationship?
Can you see how you each play your role perfectly to provide the other person an opportunity for self discovery?
Can you see the Divine nature of your conflicts?

Every argument you find yourself in can be resolved if
you're willing to take responsibility. What is responsibility?
The ability to *respond* instead of *react*. Respond to what?
The ability to respond to truth. You can learn to *respond* to
truth. You only *react* to fear. And what is truth? Truth is the
voice of wisdom within. It has been with you since the beginning of time. You hear it, whether you like it or not, and
whether you agree with it or not. The voice of conscience—
your soul, your Higher Self, your spiritual nature—never
lets you down. Walt Disney's greatest contribution to this
culture may have been his 1940 film *Pinocchio*, the story
of a living puppet who, with the help of a cricket named
Jiminy, must prove himself worthy to become a real boy.
He learns to do this by listening to his conscience...Jiminy
Cricket, who represents the voice of truth that dwells within
all of us.

A wise person once said, "Pain is the difference between
the truth I know and the action I take." Being responsible
is having the ability to respond to truth by hearing the wise
voice of conscience within and honoring it in word and
deed. If you fail to act responsibly you will wind up blaming yourself for not having honored your truth. If you don't

wind up blaming yourself, you'll wind up projecting blame on to someone else. When you do that you become the victim because when you're a victim it feels like you don't have to take responsibility. However, once you become the victim, a part of you will not let you be at peace.

There's a gift in every relationship if you take responsibility instead of blaming when upset occurs. Your relationship offers you frequent opportunities to learn to recognize and respond to an inner truth. Every relationship will put in front of you a reflection that is symbolic of your relationship with truth.

Once again, take a moment to think about the dynamics of your most recent argument. Allow your old way of being to function so that your thoughts turn to judgment and blame. What did he or she do that caused the problem? Now, stop, breathe, don't go any further; instead remember to ask the key question: Have I ever exhibited the same trait or am I capable under certain circumstances of behaving in a similar manner?

In our relationship we have found that during every argument, when we're being totally honest, we recognize in our beloved traits we also have and need to own. Ron gets impatient with Denny's impatience. Denny gets judgmental about Ron being judgmental. These reflections are not easy to spot in the heat of battle, but once a time-out has been taken, cooler heads prevail, and we go deep inside to seek the truth, we always find more similarity than difference. *If you can spot it, you've got it.*

Arguments have an energy pattern. We liken this to the pattern that is demonstrated by creating a long line of dominoes placed on end and watching what happens when you knock over the first domino. As it falls it strikes and activates the second domino, then the third and fourth and so on. Eventually hundreds of dominoes can be put in motion and tumbled by the simple act of knocking over the first domino. Preventing full scale arguments is as simple as catching them before "the first domino falls." Once the first domino is activated, it's out of your hands and the action has a life of its own. The same is true with arguments. Once set in motion they are difficult to stop. Ideally, we can learn to avoid activation by becoming conscious of what sets us in motion.

The next time you find yourself at the start of a disagreement we suggest you use a version of the Freeze Frame technique developed by the HeartMath Company of Boulder Creek, California. *Freeze the action. Stop. Call a time-out. Release your thoughts long enough to de-activate the brain and activate the heart.* You can activate the heart simply by putting your attention there. Instead of continuing thoughts about your argument, you replace them with thoughts of love. You can activate the intelligence of the heart by remembering a significant love experience. Once you've captured the feeling of love, triggered by the memory of a loved one or the memory of a loving experience...ask yourself in a very deep way, "What is really going on here?" Or, "What would be a better way of dealing with this?" The intelligence of the heart will always respond with the truth you know on a higher level. You owe it to yourself and your partner to seek out this counsel, listen to it, and respond accordingly.

Improving Communication

Decades ago we learned from the late Victor Baranco of More House in Lafayette, California, that communication has two parts.

First is speaking your truth.

Second is recognizing that it is also your responsibility to walk down the hallway between you and your partner and open your partner's door to make sure he or she receives your message.

Effective communication includes: **One:** Saying it. **Two:** Making sure it's heard.

Many fights result from: "I told him and he didn't hear me."

It is your responsibility to make sure you're heard. Do what it takes. Check to make sure the meaning of your statement is clear and has been properly understood. Ask that it be repeated back to you or acknowledged. Hang in there until your message has been validated. Yelling louder or repeating yourself does not guarantee you will be heard. Neither does judgment or accusation. The minute you use a sentence that begins with "you" (such as "you never" or "you always"), your partner will slam the door and not hear another word you say. If you want to make sure your message is heard use "I" statements, (such as "I feel" or "I think"). This takes judgment out of the statement, eliminating the need for defensive posturing, and places the responsibility on the one delivering the message. Doing this will move you closer to neutral ground, thus allowing your partner's door to open and communication to take place.

Case Building

We need to be willing to hang in there until we know we've been heard. If we quit too soon we wind up resenting the other person. Resentment leads to case building. Case building self-talk goes something like this:

"No matter what I do he just doesn't listen." Or, "She just doesn't hear me." Or, "I told him, but there he goes again."

Case building takes place in our minds. It gets embellished by our feelings of victimization. It's made real through the stories we tell ourselves and the stories we tell our sympathetic friends, even the stories we tell our therapists. Case building leads to a game that any number can play. We begin to believe that the more people we have on our side the more right we are. We become accomplished spin doctors as we repeat our cases over and over again, making them more real with each telling. Some people are so good at case building they could try their cases before the Supreme Court. The truth of the matter is, all situations are fundamentally neutral. As we said earlier: the only meaning they have is the one we assign through our beliefs and judgments formulated by our life experiences.

Becoming aware of case building moves you out of your personality/ego self, the first step toward allowing the voice of Spirit to resume its rightful place as your inner guide. Remember, when you're case building you're convincing yourself that you're right. Instead of case building, see what you experience when you ask: "Is this story I'm repeating true? How do I know it's true? Could something else be just as true?" This is another opportunity to make the choice between being right or being happy.

The most destructive consequence of Case Building happens when circumstances change in your relationship and you and your partner have resolved your differences and have reunited. Suddenly you discover that your loyal friends and family don't like your partner. You may have forgiven him/her, but they haven't. You were so convincing in building your case that they can't image how you could continue to be involved with someone who treats you so badly.

"Pleading the Case" and "This Case is Closed"

There's a similar dynamic that Denny witnesses frequently in her office while working with couples. See if you identify with this one. We call it "Pleading the Case" and "This Case is Closed." We know it well, because we've done it ourselves. Having become aware of it and called our own game, we not only do it less often now, we do it far less dramatically and with much less destructiveness. The game goes like this.

Suddenly we find ourselves in a disagreement. Communication has failed to resolve the problem and a degree of frustration has built up. It is most likely an issue that we have been through before and each one of us has a clear and undisputed viewpoint on the situation. In an effort to be understood, Denny becomes more animated, more passionate in the presentation of her side of the story. Suddenly, Ron responds by saying, "You're raising your voice. Why are you raising your voice? Don't shout at me." Once again the problem has become Denny's fault. Because she raised her voice, Ron feels justified in being done with the matter and, as far as he is concerned, the case is closed.

Denny has been passionately pleading her case, hoping to win Ron's understanding of her viewpoint. Ron, in the meantime, is convinced that no matter what Denny says, he's known the reality of the situation from the beginning of the discussion and there's nothing further to be said or done. He knows the way it is and he knows what's best. A whole generation of men exist who were conditioned to this justification by the television show "Father Knows Best." Anyhow, his mind is made up. As far as he's concerned, "The case is CLOSED." Have you ever wondered why it's so hard to get a man to stop a car he's driving to ask for directions? It's because he thinks he already knows where he's going and how to get there, or thinks he *should* know.

Try as she may during couples counseling, Denny is seldom able to head off the woman who is getting up a head of steam and is about to "Plead her case." Try as she may, Denny has seldom been able to change the male mind once he's decided, "The case is closed." Once again, we have a dynamic in which two people hold totally different perspectives and each one would rather be right than happy. The man is totally convinced that his view is the one, true, objective reality. The woman wants the man to understand and acknowledge that her reality is valid for her. Both parties are missing the point. There is no objective reality—there is no "That's the way it is." Nothing happens independent of the mind. Reality is subjective. Everything is experienced in the mind and therefore subject to the feelings and interpretations of the person thinking. Once something has happened "out there" it is taken "in here," into the mind, where subjectivity takes over, judgments are made, and opinions are formed.

The best help Denny has been able to give couples locked in this kind of disagreement is the understanding that this dynamic is fear-based rather than coming from love. As we've written before, "If it's not love (and we all know what love feels like), it's fear." When fear takes over we human beings behave in ways that are less than admirable. With the passage of time and in saner moments we are able to see a better way to behave than "Pleading the Case" and "Case Closed." Denny reminds couples that men like to feel appreciated and women like to feel understood. Notice we didn't say, "be" appreciated or "be" understood. A person can be appreciated or be understood by his or her partner, but if that person doesn't feel it, it doesn't count. Ron discovered in an interaction with Denny that the key to her feeling understood was when he switched his demeanor from "closed" to "cooperative." Once he dropped the notion that he knew best and he recognized and honored the fact that he and Denny are partners on the same team, the dynamic began to shift. How differently the situation will unfold if, when the woman's voice raises and she becomes impassioned, the man says, "Honey, help me open up as I struggle to understand where you're coming from." Doing this is like catching the first domino before it falls.

Denny has learned a very effective way to allow a man to feel appreciated. The key is how you say it. The words we recommend are: "I really appreciate the way you _____" (fill in the blank with whatever it is you appreciate). It must be done in these words, which connect with the masculine left brain. If it's done in the traditional flowery, intuitive, right brain female style it simply doesn't register in the left brain male. Likewise, how different the situation will be if the woman recognizes that the male mind has shut and "The case is closed." Once the case is closed, banging on the door won't make it open. Persuasive arguments, brilliant examples, and pearls of wisdom fall on deaf ears. The situation will only change if she slows down and gently says, "I really appreciate where you're coming from. And I appreciate that you're having difficulty understanding my position. Maybe we can talk about this later when we're not so stuck."

It is our belief and it has been our experience that everything that happens to us happens for a reason. When seen from a larger perspective, everything offers us a blessing. What might the blessing be in this "Case Closed" dynamic? What opportunity has been presented here for us to learn a spiritual lesson? In our case, it was an opportunity to learn to manage the harmonious flow of our energy to create the positive reality we prefer. In the process of overcoming our destructive behavior we realized that during this kind of disagreement we were both shutting down our flow of energy. We were allowing our personal vibratory frequencies to decrease during these storms of negativity, when what was needed to solve our problem was to raise our vibratory frequency to a higher level. Our goal is to have a harmonious and loving relationship and to grow together as Spiritual partners. We know this happens only when we each maintain positive, high vibratory frequencies. Whenever a situation develops and Denny feels

Ron is not understanding her viewpoint, the combination of passion and frustration that she builds up is extremely constrictive to her flow of energy. Think of your energy as traveling through a pipe or channel, which is you. When she starts pleading her case the pipeline is constricted by the pressure of the passion. The channel to her energetic flow is not opening—it's closing. The same situation occurs in Ron. As he reacts to Denny by thinking he knows the reality of the situation and decides that "This case is closed," his channel crimps his energy flow. As we wrote in our previous book, what you put out is what you get back. A closing down of energy by one partner will be matched by a closing down of energy by the other partner.

The good news is: Ron and Denny haven't engaged in the "Case Closed" dynamic in a long time. We consider it a blessing to have been able to witness our destructive actions and see that they were detrimental to our relationship. Remembering our commitment to Spiritual partnership and being willing to figure out what was behind the dynamic so we could both make another choice was a blessing. If you don't like it, you can change it, but you have to want happiness more than being right. We both consider our revelation and subsequent course correction a huge step forward in our Spiritual growth. Before closing this chapter we'd like to point out that "Pleading the Case" is not exclusive to women and "Case Closed" is not exclusive to men. These behaviors are interchangeable, and no matter who's playing which role, the dynamic is destructive *and* the situation offers an opportunity for change and growth.

If all this processing seems overwhelming to you, there is a much quicker solution to resolving this relationship dynamic. The shortcut is: just let go. For the woman, stop trying to plead your case. Just let it go. For the man, stop your stubborn mindset and just let it go. In the midst of writing this chapter we stopped for lunch at a Chinese restaurant. Spirit spoke to us in the form of a fortune cookie that read, "Learning to shrug is the first step to wisdom."

CHAPTER EIGHT

Playing with the Tar Baby

Sticky conflicts occur when we continue to argue for the rightness of our position. These conflicts complicate our relationships. We call this complication "Playing with the Tar Baby." The feelings of your partner become unimportant compared to your need to be right. Painful words are exchanged and each partner becomes more and more stuck and polarized, determined to win.

Remember, the secret to a successful relationship is understanding that everything we experience is a reflection of our inner reality. If we are having conflict in our inner reality the Tar Baby Game becomes our outer experience. Just like Brear Rabbit in *The Tales of Uncle Remus*, when you play with the Tar Baby, you're going to get stuck. You may not even know how you got there.

Let's take a look at what happens when a couple that's been happily married for 45 years suddenly find themselves in a sticky disagreement. We consider ourselves to be a fairly conscious couple, happy most of the time. We are generally kind to each other, enjoy each other, respect each other and are very loving with each other. So what rocks the boat?

Here we are in Sedona, Arizona, at the end of a wonderful eight day vacation surrounded by people we love and enjoy, having a good time. We've said good-bye to our vacation week visitors and have thanked our friends who live in Sedona for once again providing so many happy moments during our week-long stay. We depart, saying after such a busy week we need some "alone time." We jokingly call it our "SFT: Special Fight Time." Be careful what you say. Twenty minutes later we're at Safeway picking up a bottle of wine to take back to our motel room for our final night in Sedona and we begin to create a reality that is the direct result of our SFT remark.

From Ron's Perspective

As I'm making the wine selection, it dawns on me that I don't know whether or not we have a corkscrew. We had just spent seven days in a timeshare condominium that was fully equipped, including a wine bottle opener that I'd been using all week. It occurs to me that since we'd moved to a motel room for our final night, I might not have a corkscrew to open the wine bottle, so I ask Denny if she knows whether we have one or not.

Denny can't understand why I'm even concerned. In her mind we always have a corkscrew when we're traveling. An unpleasant disagreement erupts as we proceed to discuss whether or not we need to buy a corkscrew. Our relationship begins to get sticky and the Tar Baby Game is underway. We become like two ships passing in the night. We are suddenly in two very different worlds. I can't understand her certainty that we have a corkscrew. She can't understand why I'm worried that we might not have one.

As I stand in the checkout line, Denny goes to the car to look in our suitcases. She reports back to me that we do indeed have a wine opener and we don't need to buy one. By this time the rapport between us has become strained and tense, but we both cool down enough to prevent the situation from escalating from a minor disagreement into a full blown argument. It just remains sticky and uncomfortable. Neither one of us is willing to totally let go of our position.

From Denny's Perspective

I was exhausted. We had been with friends constantly. I was now on overload and I just wanted to collapse in our motel room and be quiet. We stopped at Safeway to pick up some wine for the evening. Suddenly Ron turned to me and asked in a startled voice, "Do we have a corkscrew?" I tried to understand what he was asking me. We have carried a corkscrew in our overnight bag for the past ten to fifteen years. It was removed one time when we went through airport security and we replaced it immediately. The question made no sense to me. I assumed that Ron was concerned that perhaps he had removed the corkscrew from the bag. I said to him, "Gee, I saw you using a corkscrew at the condo." His reply was, "That was the corkscrew that belonged to the condo." Then I asked, "Why would you think the corkscrew wasn't in the overnight bag?" He replied, "Well I didn't know which bags we brought. You were deciding between two bags and I didn't know if you brought the one with the corkscrew."

That's when I became annoyed and suddenly I was stuck with the Tar Baby.

❦

This was a tiny disagreement, hardly worth bothering about. But what happens in a relationship when you get several of these minor disagreements and you don't resolve them? They pile up and resentment piles up with them. It's like finding ants. If you don't deal with the first one, before long you have an army of them. Becoming conscious of your part in minor squabbles is like preventive medicine. If you can resolve it right away, major rifts can be avoided.

Sometimes disagreements erupt because energy has built up and needs to be released, much like the weather when a storm gathers momentum and eventually dissipates. Sometimes disagreements occur because we allow ourselves to get too tired or cranky. Alcoholic's Anonymous uses the acronym HALT to address this issue. Don't get too Hungry, Angry, Lonely, or Tired. It is at such times that we can easily become unconscious. On the other hand, we've learned that there are no accidents. Every event occurs to provide an opportunity for the soul's growth. By challenging our beliefs we reduce our need to play the destructive Tar Baby Game. If we seek the truth, the truth will set us free. We have found that the ultimate truth is that the argument is not about the other person. It is a blessing that allows us to find another aspect of ourselves that needs to be brought to consciousness, embraced, and loved.

When you get stuck, here are some things you can do. In the midst of the fear, anxiety, panic or turmoil of the Tar

Baby Game it's helpful to call a "time-out" and once again engage in honest self-inquiry. Ask yourself:

What is my part in this conflict?

What do I believe about my partner?

What do I believe about myself?

Did I behave in a less than desirable manner because I was afraid?

The answers to all four of these questions can help you return to your center. Repeat that important pledge:

"I create my own reality. I am not a victim."

CHAPTER NINE

Trust and Truth: Where to Begin

All relationships succeed or fail in direct proportion to the amount of trust and truth they embody. All lasting relationships are anchored here, on a foundation of trust and truth. You can't have one without the other. In fact, the two are so intertwined that it is difficult to separate them, even for this discussion. Let's start with *Webster's New World Dictionary* definitions. Trust is defined as: "Firm belief in the honesty and reliability, etc. of another." Truth is defined as: "Sincerity; honesty...conformity with fact."

The first step to establishing trust in a relationship is cultivating the ability to trust yourself. What does it mean to trust yourself? Trusting yourself means meeting your self commitments. If you say, "I will exercise tomorrow," then you need to get up and exercise. If you don't, your words are meaningless and you can't begin to trust that you will do what you say. If you're constantly rationalizing and you don't allow yourself to deal with what you're feeling in a straightforward manner, there is no basis for self-trust. If you refuse to confront painful situations when they arise, how can you possibly believe that others are telling *you* the truth about what *they're* experiencing? If you refuse to take responsibility and own your part in an interaction, how can you believe anyone else would own their part?

Another aspect of trusting yourself is cultivating the ability to tell the whole truth, without either enhancing or diminishing details of your behavior. We judge and interpret the behavior of others based on what we would do in similar circumstances. If we're less than impeccable we'll never be able to believe another. You must keep your side of a relationship perfectly clean. It is only then that you can begin to trust others. We can't overemphasize the importance of first working on yourself.

There is an element that makes a huge contribution to the establishment of trust. That element is truth. And the first step to truthfulness is telling *yourself* the truth. If you know that you don't always speak the truth, you're not going to believe what others tell you. People often have a hard time telling the truth to themselves because it evokes uncomfortable feelings, feelings that are unpopular or unwanted. Nevertheless, it's not what the truth is that matters: it's telling it. One person may think that their truth is the most horrible truth imaginable. They may have a terminal illness and not want to share the horror of their reality. Yet to establish a close and loving relationship with another human being, they have to share that truth. Once the truth is shared and acknowledged, the doors open to the possibility of a real and meaningful relationship.

Do you have the courage to speak your truth? Have you cultivated the ability to discern facts, to see the truth? Or are you seduced by the story the ego comes up with to feed its own interests? These ego-generated stories do not equal the truth. They're just the stories we tell to make ourselves right, while making someone else wrong. Our story is made up by the ego to hide our unconscious Shadow aspects. Our story is the spin we put on circumstances to fit our needs. Strangely enough, the ego will sometimes come up with a story that portrays us as a hero or "better than," and other times the ego will make us feel "less than," like a victim in need of pity.

To really appreciate how prevalent people's stories are, we recommend you do a little eavesdropping. Listen to the conversations that are going on around you. People are always telling their stories, especially the folks talking on their cell phones. They even tell their stories at a louder volume to make sure they're heard. Once you become adept at recognizing other people's stories, start observing your own conversations and notice what stories you tell. As you do this, try to stay conscious. Remember your story is not reality: it's just your interpretation of the situation.

In addition to the stories we tell others, there are the stories we tell ourselves, our internal dialogue, the running commentary that interprets everything we experience. It's like we each have our own play-by-play announcer. But this unending commentary from the voice in our heads does not equal the truth. It is important to realize that this internal dialogue is also the ego's interpretation of people and events.

Write Your Story

Get a pencil and paper. Recall a recurring disagreement that tarnishes one of your significant relationships. Listen to your own play-by-play announcer describe your situation. When the details are clearly in focus, write your story. What is it you're experiencing? What is your interpretation of your partner's actions? What is he/she thinking, feeling, and meaning? What are you thinking, feeling, and meaning?

◎/◎

Getting conscious is a two step process. First, you have to recognize that you have created a story. Second, you have to look closely at what you're saying to see if it's valid or just your rationalization. Is it true or do you just *think* it's true? What are you trying to cover up or avoid that is keeping you from seeing yourself clearly? This is difficult to do alone, which is why we learn so much about ourselves when we examine our stories in the context of our most significant relationships. When you're in a relationship it becomes extremely important to spot the difference between interpretation and truth. Are you reporting the facts or spinning the story?

Sometimes when we interpret, we're simply trying to make sense of the unusual behavior of those around us. This is especially true of men and women, baffled by each other's actions. Instead of interpreting, it is possible to learn to ask those we're involved with to tell us what is going on. "What is the meaning of your words? What is the meaning of your action?" In a healthy relationship, first you ask the other person for the truth and then you accept what they tell you, rather than believing the story you have been telling yourself. This only works when you can trust the other person to tell the truth. Remember, your Shadow may be at work here. You will not trust others if there's an unrecognized part of you that is not always trustworthy. You will not trust the truth of other people's stories, if your stories don't ring true. In order to trust yourself, you need to make an inner commitment to reveal the truth. This means if you are unhappy, you must say so. If your feelings are hurt, you must be forthcoming. What you need to get in order to trust another person, you must be willing to give. If you expect your partner to keep time commitments, you must also be punctual. If you expect fidelity, you too must be faithful. Give what you need to get.

The old way of establishing trust in a relationship was to get to know someone, decide you really liked them, decide you loved them and then you gave them your trust. Later, if they began to behave in ways you didn't understand, you could decide you didn't like that behavior and justify pulling back a piece of your trust. If this happened more than once you might have eventually pulled away all of your trust and been left with only your interpretation, and no relationship.

The new way of establishing trust is to figure out what it would take for the other person to *earn* your trust. This requires a commitment to honest communication, being absolutely straight with each other. For example, to earn Denny's trust she needs those she's involved with to share their feelings with her as honestly as they can. She needs to have people tell her what they like and don't like. She needs to be told no, when the answer is no. Trying to be nice or placating her creates distance. She needs people to say what they mean and mean what they say. If Ron says he'll be home at five o'clock, she needs him to arrive on time or call to say he'll be late. She needs to know that

her feelings will be taken seriously and dealt with respect-
fully. When these criteria have been met consistently over
time, trust is earned. When trust has been earned it can't
be pulled away. You don't get to interpret the other person's
behavior. If something seems amiss you have to check it
out rather than making up stories or becoming a victim.
Giving the other person an opportunity to tell you what
transpired saves both of you unnecessary hurt and pain.

The ultimate relationship would be one where there
was no need for this kind of "check it out communication."
This is eventually possible when the highest level of trust
has been established between two people, because there is
no further need for interpretation or clarification. When
someone has earned our trust, we tell him the truth. When
we have earned someone else's trust, she tells us the truth.
Once truth is on the table, interpretation is no longer needed. It is replaced by love; and truth and love are synony-
mous. In any given situation we always have two paths
before us. We can choose to interpret the event, which we
usually do in our heads, or we can function at a higher
level and simply understand the truth of the matter, which
is done with the heart, and not with the head.

Before his death in 1986, our dear friend Mike Bippus
shared with us these inspired words of wisdom about interpretation and understanding that he received in a medita-
tive state:

"Interpretation gone unsaid…understand instead…I did."

In other words, if we don't succumb to the voice of the
ego that takes us down the path of interpretation and story
telling, we can simply allow ourselves to understand, and

this means listening to our hearts for the truth of what is going on.

⚭

We cannot overemphasize the important role truth plays in every relationship. The lack of truth is the greatest menace to trust. For example, a couple is watching the Sunday football game on television. He says, "Are you having a good time?"

She says, "Yeah, this is great." But inside she's thinking, "Can't he see I'm miserable? Doesn't he know I don't like football?"

He's drinking beer and loving the game. She's bored and would rather go somewhere. She's not happy, but afraid to say so. He takes her at her word and believes she's having as good a time as he is. He's maintaining the trust that she will be forthcoming, but she is not and the relationship suffers.

Another example: She finds a Kleenex in his coat pocket with lipstick on it. She asks if he's having an affair. He denies it. She accepts him at his word. She's keeping her side of the relationship clean by coming from truth and trust. If he's not telling the truth, he then has to live with the consequences of having lied to someone who loves and trusts him. He also has to live with the consequence of having lost his inner sense of well-being. No amount of rationalizing on his part can obscure the truth he knows in his heart. A man who's willing to cheat or lie puts the relationship at risk and damages the sacred relationship he has with himself as well. That lie will eventually eat him alive and in time will be revealed. The classic example is Bill Clinton's Monica Lewinsky lie of 1998.

For the woman, the betrayal and heartbreak of infidelity is also an opportunity to go inside and ask, "Why would I be involved with someone who would cheat and lie? What is this reflecting to me? Where did I not trust myself?"

Learning of an affair seems to come as a shock and surprise, but on some level it's not. We always know. Affairs are symptoms of a problem...and not the real problem or issue. In relationship the real issue lies within. What part of one's inner reality does an affair reflect? Perhaps it's the belief that everyone cheats, so I've chosen a partner willing to validate my belief. Maybe we're unconsciously following an energy pattern in the family. "Dad cheated on Mom, what else can I expect?" Maybe deep inside, we are afraid to be alone and so we won't allow ourselves to know of this betrayal. Or we think we can't survive without a partner, so we'll tolerate anything to stay in the relationship. Most of the stories we tell ourselves are created to soothe a frightened inner child—that part of us that was hurt in childhood and is still carrying the scar. Our journey from childhood to adulthood can be seen as the journey from scared to sacred. Each word has the same letters, slightly rearranged...s-c-a-r-e-d and s-a-c-r-e-d. We're always on that fine line between scared and sacred, between choosing illusion and truth, between fear and love. When we are afraid, it has helped us to think of the "c-a" in scared as standing for "child afraid." We also like to think of the "a-c" in sacred as standing for "adult conscious."

In your relationships you will constantly be given opportunities to choose between love and fear... to speak your truth or hedge with a lie...to be the "child afraid" or the "adult conscious," to be scared or sacred. You have this opportunity in every interaction in every relationship. None will be as meaningful to the growth of your soul as the perspective you choose in the interactions with your partner. Will you choose love or fear?

Getting from Scared to Sacred

We know of three helpful ways to get from scared to sacred in a relationship. First, don't try to educate your partner during an argument. Part of trusting is accepting that what someone says is true—is true for them. Do not try to argue them out of how they feel. Even when your partner is playing victim, even when they have fallen asleep and are not taking responsibility for creating their reality, be respectful of their process. It's impossible to enlighten or even educate during an argument. You're both caught in defending yourselves and neither of you will be able to be truthful in the midst of your quest to be right. Cool off, call a time-out. Perhaps at some later time, when neither of you is feeling defensive or fearful, you can go back and carefully explore from a loving perspective what was going on. In doing so, check things out, once again making sure that both your words and intention are properly understood. It is disrespectful to believe the story you tell yourself, rather than the words coming from your partner. You don't know them better than they know themselves. You don't live in their skin. They are separate individuals with a perspective just as valid as yours. Speak your truth, listen, and trust.

Second, as we mentioned earlier, it helps to make

friends with your Shadow parts, and even name them. This will help you to understand these traits in other people. For example, once you discover you don't like someone else's stubbornness, recognize and claim your own stubbornness. Value the gifts you get from your stubbornness. See how it has helped you be tenacious and determined to reach your goals. Learn to love and appreciate your stubbornness for what it does for you. The benefit of nicknaming your stubbornness, such as Stubborn Sam, is that it helps you to be much lighter about that aspect of yourself, and less defensive. Once you stop being defensive, you can begin appreciating and you'll find that the situation can be discussed with your partner in a far less threatening manner. So when your partner is exhibiting unpleasant traits, lovingly and playfully check it out. Don't accuse or pronounce, but inquire, "Was Bitchy Brenda here today?" When the trait is not personalized in a negative, judgmental way, it's easier to talk about.

The third way to get from scared to sacred in your relationship is to check out your beliefs, especially the invisible ones. If you say, "That's just the way it is," or "That's just the way I am," it's a sign that an invisible belief is operating. Invisible beliefs are beliefs we have that we don't realize we have. We have usually inherited them from our culture, parents, teachers, friends or other loved ones, rather than chosen them deliberately. Invisible beliefs are also ones that no longer serve us.

For example, men and women usually have totally different attitudes about investments based on their invisible beliefs. When an investment goes sour, a man tends to see it as the fault of the company he has invested in. He'll say something like, "Gee the stock looked good when I bought it. Too bad the company failed, but I had no way of knowing." Women, on the other hand, tend to see it as their fault. A woman might say, "I really made a bad decision when I chose that stock. If only I had picked a better stock."

In our opinion the patriarchy, a culture ruled by men, has been perpetuated through invisible beliefs that do not serve or promote loving relationships. When there's something wrong, the patriarchy promotes the view that it must be "her fault." This dynamic can be traced all the way back to Adam and Eve in the Garden of Eden. Both men and women have unfortunately bought this line of thinking. In order to control the situation women have learned to say, "Yes, it's my fault and if only I could change, everything would be better." Men agree, because it lets them off the hook and they can say, "I'm not responsible; if only she were different it wouldn't have happened." If this is beginning to sound familiar, perhaps you and your partner have the same default positions that we've already acknowledged we have. Our patriarchal culture promotes such beliefs and makes them seem like that's just the way it is.

CHAPTER TEN

Uncovering Hidden Beliefs

As we have mentioned, there are two powerful forces that take turns driving relationships. These two forces are love and fear. The quality of a relationship is determined by which force we permit to take charge. It is as simple as this: when we come from a loving perspective we experience a loving and harmonious relationship. When we come from a fear-based perspective we experience friction, discontent, disharmony and all manner of upset. These fear-based behaviors come in a variety of forms. We've picked some common examples. Notice that each example is driven by an underlying invisible belief that has a negative impact on the relationship.

Because we live in a patriarchal, fear-based society, there is a male-female game that springs from a deep-seated invisible belief that tarnishes many relationships. It's a belief some men picked up as boys. It has a very crude name but it's important to confront it so you know what we're dealing with.

Pussy Whipped

Although you won't find "pussy whipped" in the diction-ary, most men reading this book will be familiar with the expression, which they probably first heard in elementary or middle school. It was the worst thing a boy could be in those hormone-driven days of early puberty. When young boys were experiencing their first crush on a girl, their male peers were on guard to make sure they didn't loose their masculinity. The peer group did this by teasing, harassing, and constantly challenging all male responses to requests by the female. Falling in love was okay, but being taken over by your girlfriend was not. At this stage of develop-ment adolescent boys don't have a sense of Self, but they know that they don't want to be their girlfriend's puppet. They learn to fear having their strings pulled by a female puppeteer. And so every sign of a boy doing anything in response to a feminine request was seen as giving up mas-culine control, failing to be macho...or in other words, be-ing pussy whipped.

Many men have unknowingly carried this syndrome into their adult partnerships and even their marriages. That's how indelible a mark it made in the lives of young men coming of age who just wanted to be accepted as "one of the guys." It is one of those terrible invisible beliefs that was accepted by default in childhood and lives on in adult-hood. This invisible fear of being pussy whipped plays a highly subversive role in many relationships.

Men need to ask themselves how many times they have purposely *not* done something she wanted so they wouldn't feel pussy whipped. Has this enhanced or dimished your relationship? What would your life be like if you gave in? What if you didn't care whether or not you were pussy whipped?

A variation of pussy whipped that is much more subtle occurs in the dynamic of a man and woman discussing what she wants. Let's say they're talking about where she wants to go for dinner. She says she wants a hamburger. He decides he wants to take her out for lobster. He'll look better, feel better, and be in control if he spends big and makes it "special." They go for the lobster, but at some point she reminds him she really just wanted a hamburger. He resents her for not appreciating his generosity and the expensive lobster dinner. She, on the other hand, feels she never gets what she wants. She feels unheard and unimportant.

It is vital to recognize that there are two ways of giving. One is giving the other person what *you want* to give them. The second way is giving them what *they want*. There's room in most relationships for both ways of giving, but men need to recognize when it's time to give the second way to avoid resentment and discontent.

Women also play their part in setting this dynamic in motion. When women get caught up in romance, they believe their partners should instinctively know what they want without having to tell them. But when they're given the wrong thing, women become irritated, sometimes even enraged. This is one dark side or Shadow side of romance. So men need to learn to listen to women. And women need to take responsibility for saying what they really want.

Ask the Vagina

Ironically, many of the same men who struggle not to be pussy whipped think nothing of participating in another strange scenario we call "Ask the Vagina." Without giving it any conscious thought many men, Ron included, rely upon their female partners to know answers to questions like, "Where are my brown socks?" Ask the Vagina.

"What's that noise?" Ask the Vagina.

"Where's the scotch tape?" Ask the Vagina.

"What do I want for lunch?" Ask the Vagina.

"What are we doing this weekend?" Ask the Vagina.

"When's my next doctor's appointment?" Ask the Vagina.

Ask the Vagina sounds a lot like the questions little boys ask their mommies.

It is time that men, who won't allow themselves to be pussy whipped, cop to the fact that they are the same men who are turning to the women in their lives asking for answers to these pressing questions. And men can't have it both ways. They can't rebel for fear of being pussy whipped and then turn around and Ask the Vagina.

The Ask the Vagina phenomenon exists in more than just marriage relationships. If men aren't asking their wives, they're asking their mothers. If they're not asking their mothers, they're asking their administrative assistants. It seems to have become a universally accepted belief that women have a special honing device in their vaginas that keeps track of where everything is at any given time. This same device also knows where to buy things, where to find things in a grocery store, when social engagements are coming up. Every detail of organized life seems to be contained in that magic compartment...the vagina.

She Has Him Wrapped around Her Little Finger

While many men allow the invisible fear of being pussy whipped to tarnish their adult relationships with women, a number of women carry an invisible belief that is also damaging their relationships with men. It is the negative belief that women need to manipulate to get what they want from men. Women learn this manipulation process in order to survive in the patriarchy. When women feel they can't stand up to the powerful domination of the patriarchy, they're driven underground and for their survival they learn to manipulate. It is a self-preservation technique women learn in order to charm the captor to get what they want, much the same way the hostages taken captive at the American Embassy in Tehran, Iran, did in 1979 in order to stay alive. It's also similar to Patty Hearst's survival behavior after she was kidnapped by the Symbionese Liberation Army in 1974. This behavior is known as the Stockholm Syndrome, named for an event involving four people who were taken hostage in Stockholm, Sweden, in the summer of 1973. At the end of their six days of captivity they actively resisted rescue and then refused to testify against their captors, even raising money for their captors' defense. Experts explain that the Stockholm Syndrome comes into play when a kidnap victim cannot escape and is isolated and threatened with death, but at the same time receives some acts of kindness from the captors. The syndrome also helps us understand the behavior of battered spouses, religious cult victims and Holocaust survivors. While women surviving the patriarchy have not literally been kidnapped, some feel they are just as powerless as if they had been.

The problem with female manipulation in an intimate relationship is that it winds up harming the manipulator. It harms her because she can never trust that what she is getting from the male is genuine. She will always question whether it was freely given or whether she got it because she manipulated for it. Furthermore, it is disrespectful to the male partner because the underlying belief that justifies manipulation is that men are stupid and if women pull the right strings they can get men to do whatever they want them to do. When you "have him wrapped around your little finger," you've come full circle from his fear of being pussy whipped to your expressing manipulating, pussy whipping behavior.

The Fragile Male Ego

Opposite from the belief that men are powerful, but stupid; is the invisible belief that men are inherently weak and have fragile egos. There are dozens of things that women do or don't do and say or don't say because of this belief. Women walk on egg shells to avoid disturbing the fragile male ego. Women who believe that men have fragile egos do not tell them the truth. They rationalize that since men can't deal with the truth, there's no point in bothering to tell it. Countless women believe if they want something done they have to do it themselves—that you can't count on men because they either won't do it, or they won't do it right. They may have been taught this belief directly by their mothers or other women in their family. They may have picked up the concept more subtly through role modeling, observing the subversive way mother handled father as the child was growing up. The unspoken belief that men are the weaker sex pervades our culture. We see it on television shows and in movies in which the man is portrayed as unable to cope with the truth and must be protected from it by the female, or when the male ego is buttered-up and stroked to enable the female to do as she pleases. When women believe that men are fragile it gives them permission to keep secrets. Women then feel justified in not telling men the whole truth. They pull their punches because they believe the fragile male ego will not be able to deal with the reality of their feelings.

For example, the man may say, "I'd like us to visit my family this weekend."

The woman responds, "That would be nice, but I've got a lot to do, so let's make it a short visit." Her internal dialogue is more likely to be: "He's forgotten again what a struggle I have with his mother. If I remind him he'll get that hurt look on his face and pout. The only thing I can do now is pretend I'm enjoying myself. He owes me one."

In a more honest relationship, where there are no games, the wife could say, "Honey remember—your mom and I don't always get along. It's difficult for me to spend time with her. If we go this weekend, I'll need your help and understanding."

The first response, which stems from a negative, invisible belief and is fear-based, will eventually lead to problems. Chances are a blow-out fight will erupt before the weekend is over. The second response, based in love and truth, is an opportunity for the couple to draw closer. Remember, it's not the content of the truth that matters—it's speaking it that counts.

A more subtle form of the belief that men have fragile egos is the way that society treats the bully. It is common knowledge that a bully does not feel good about himself and that's why he picks on others. A bully attempts to get his good feelings at the expense of those around him. The idea that "boys will be boys" and that the fragile male ego needs to be stroked can be seen when teachers on the playground do not intervene during bullying situations. Furthermore, we accept that politicians have the right to bully their opponents. We live in a culture where it's believed that one country has the right to bully another country. It is no wonder that women find it difficult to hold their men accountable when the men become bullies. The myth of the fragile male ego tolerates and perpetuates inappropriate male behavior. Bullying, carried to an extreme, can become spousal abuse. How many wife beatings have resulted from women allowing men to bully them because they believed they had no right to expect a higher standard of behavior from the fragile male ego?

Invisible beliefs that lead to these behaviors are very destructive. Whenever we withhold our truth from our partner a conflict is sure to arise. Whenever we treat the other, whether male or female, as incapable or inferior, our relationship will be in trouble. These negative ways of relating are so prevalent in our culture that we often say that's just the way it is, and we don't attempt to see beyond our fear-based invisible, destructive, disrespectful beliefs. When we learn to treat the other as an equal partner we open the door to a healthy, long-lasting relationship.

Parents have an incredible opportunity, whether they're raising sons or daughters, to break the cycle. Parents have the power, if not the obligation, to teach their sons to take a higher path. Similarly they can teach their daughters to respect their male partners, rather than catering to the myth of the fragile male ego. This can be done either by direct instruction or by example through their own family relationships based on trust and truth.

Relationships Are Always Equal

In our experience, if one person is prone to playing one of these fear-based games, he or she will attract someone who will play the other side of the game. In other words, a man who fears he might be pussy whipped will most likely find himself attracted to a manipulative woman who is also coming from a place of fear, afraid that she can't get what she wants by simply asking for it, so she winds up manipulating. A woman who withholds the truth because she believes that men have fragile egos will find herself in a relationship with a man who doesn't share his feelings. Our early teacher about relationships, Victor Baranco, taught us that relationships are always equal. You can never have a White Knight without also having a Damsel in Distress. What roles do you and your partner play?

☙❧

Even after forty-five years of marriage, we find ourselves

with unresolved issues. Sometimes we fall into old behavior patterns and are unable to see our hidden beliefs. But the reality is—we'd rather argue with each other than spend time apart with a different partner. In Denny's practice she often asks the client who complains about a partner, "Does he/she give you enough otherwise?"

Ahhh, if the world only had someone with a larger perspective who could stand over us, see the bigger picture and wisely observe to the man, "Your life would get better if you stopped resisting requests from the female."

And standing over the female, the observer might say, "Your life would get better if you'd let go of your need to control."

The way to end all games is to wake up and become authentic. Choose love, and choose love again. From your centered Self you can find your sense of well being. You can get in touch with who you are and what you need. In becoming authentic and telling the truth you can begin to trust your partner also to tell the truth. When we're able to do this the game is over. The hidden beliefs have been exposed. Truth has returned. Love has won.

CHAPTER ELEVEN

Lasting Partnerships

Relationships make the world go around. The search for connection with that special one in your life begins at an early age. For some it begins in preschool when two children connect and become inseparable; or maybe it's that kiss in grammar school when your heart flutters for the first time. The search continues throughout the life cycle. We hear stories about those cute old couples who find each other in their retirement communities or nursing homes. What is it we're looking for? In the early stages it's romance that brings us together. Without that special chemistry we aren't attracted to each other. However, romance should not be confused with love. It's impossible to sustain a romantic connection for any significant period of time when you live together and share the day-to-day struggles of work and a family. What is it that grows in the place of romance that can sustain and nourish two people for a lifetime? We've discovered it's a special kind of friendship. Loving each other isn't enough. You have to like each other...a lot. You have to like each other enough to always choose that person to play with. There can't be any other person you'd rather be with, fight with, and share with than the person who is your partner. It's not that you have no other friends or people you associate with; it's just that you enjoy each other the very most.

There is a major difference between sharing and owning. Time shared needs to be mutually agreed upon. Neither partner has the right to own or control the other. We each get one life to live and only one. You are responsible for your choices only and have no right to dictate another's.

Hanging in There

The secret to a long-term relationship is two-fold. First, you have to learn to get over your ego self. *Don't take things personally. It's not about you.* Second, you have to come to a place where you have appreciation, tolerance, love and compassion for the peccadilloes of the person with whom you share your life.

One of the major things we've learned in sharing a life together is that our relationship is not a fifty-fifty proposition. It's one hundred percent/one hundred percent. If it's fifty-fifty and Denny's giving her fifty percent but Ron isn't, then half of the relationship is left uncovered. On the other hand, if Denny is giving a full one hundred percent even though Ron is only giving fifty percent, the relationship is still covered one hundred percent. This means a person must take total responsibility for what occurs in the relationship regardless of whether or not the other partner does. It doesn't work to say, "I'll give when he gives." That's equivalent to looking into a mirror and saying, "I'll smile if my reflection smiles first."

We all want to be acknowledged, to be heard, to be understood, to be appreciated, to be accepted and to be loved. Since all relationships are a reflection of an inner reality, the question becomes: "In what ways do I give those things to myself?" Do you take time to acknowledge yourself and the good and loving things you do? Do you remember to praise yourself for a job well done? Many successful people don't stop to appreciate their successes. When one goal is reached they move right on to the next. They don't know how to slow down and enjoy the accomplishment. They just move quickly on to the next thing without taking time for themselves.

Denny's Story

I was working full time as a teacher for severely emotionally disturbed children when I decided to go to graduate school to pursue my dream of becoming a Marriage and Family Therapist. My youngest son was in high school and the eldest was in college. There was finally time for me. The first year, I attended graduate school part time while continuing to teach. All the while I was itching to get on with a new career. I made a major decision. I took a leave of absence from the teaching position and went to graduate school full time. This was no easy task. I had classes to attend, papers to write, tests to take and I was still a full-time wife and mother. My excitement and enthusiasm for my new career kept me going. I was able to complete my master's program in two and a half years, which was quite an accomplishment. I was anxious to move forward and decided it was unnecessary to attend graduation. After all, I was an adult in my mid-forties, why should I bother to attend a long, boring graduation ceremony when I already had what I wanted, which was my degree? When I look back now, I realize how I cheated myself. The ritual of graduation would have allowed me to honor my hard work and accomplishment.

◎/◎

Giving to yourself is a guarantee that your needs will always be met. Who knows you better than you do? If you wait around for your partner to meet all your needs, there will be times when you'll feel empty. Giving to yourself is a guarantee that you will be heard, understood, appreciated, accepted and loved. Denny has had more than one client in therapy complain about not being heard while at the same time she is ignoring her own inner guidance. You can't expect to be heard if you, yourself, are not listening. You cannot expect to be loved if you are not loving yourself. You cannot expect anyone to do for you what you will not do for yourself.

Having said this, we're eager to emphasize how important it is to remember to say sweet and loving things to your partner. As a therapist Denny works with all kinds of women who long to hear their partner say, "I love you...I care about you...and you are wonderful."

Denny usually asks them if they remember to say these things to their partner. Once again, if you're waiting and deciding you'll say it once he says it, that doesn't work anymore than deciding you'll smile only after the person in the mirror smiles. Saying those tender words so that you'll get a tender response doesn't work either. That's manipulating—giving to get. It has to be a genuine opening of the heart. When something strikes you that's tender or opens your heart, or when something about the other person moves you, it will be a bonding experience to share it, to be vulnerable, to let the other know how much you love and care. That puts you in the center of the flow of love. If you share this during the good times of your relationship it will help sustain you during the not so good times. It's the little good things that keep a relationship together. It's also the little bad things that create problems in a relationship. So, be conscious of the little things.

It is also important to learn to take each other for granted. This may sound contrary to everything you've been told about romance and making the other person feel special, so let us explain. Romance may be fun, but when you can take someone for granted it means you can trust them. It means you're secure in your love. Enjoy being in an ordinary relationship. Take each other for granted. Trust that love is there and you can count on it. You'll find it grows. On the contrary, if you're focused on the need to be special, then you're believing that you're not *really* loved. You're believing that something is lacking and a need to feel special becomes your way to make up for what isn't really there.

CHAPTER TWELVE

Issues through the Ages

Over the years, through our twenties, thirties, forties, fifties, and sixties, we have encountered unique circumstances that have challenged our relationship. What we did in our twenties was very different from what we're doing in our sixties. Our goals and the people we relate to are very different. What has remained consistent is our relationship. This primary relationship has remained fresh and growing for over forty-five years. You can create a new relationship for each decade and for every moment so long as you're willing to grow and change together.

Each decade has its built-in challenges. Our goal was to make it through the challenges with the same person, rather than having a new partner every ten years. To do this successfully takes commitment. In marriage, two people make a commitment to grow together. Instead of wanting to live happily ever after, it's important to learn how to live through the unhappy times—the times when it's not fun. When we learn to do that, we evolve.

In our twenties Ron was establishing his radio and television career. Denny was graduating from college and having babies. Our biggest challenge was learning to live with each other. We each had our unique ways of performing household tasks, dealing with money, establishing our priorities and meeting our commitments. It was a time of putting together two unique and distinct life streams. It was a time of learning to balance and integrate our individual family rituals, life styles, quirks and habits. Not only were we figuring out how to dance with each other moment to moment and day to day, we were challenged with raising children, establishing roots in a community, learning to get along with each other's families, and acquiring the necessities for comfortable survival, including a house, car, and furniture. All this adjustment was a monumental task. Every couple faces this daunting challenge of transitioning from starry eyed romance to the realities and necessities of everyday life. To this day, Denny remembers she never cried more in her life than she did during our first year of marriage. The fantasy and the reality of married life did not add up and she felt vulnerable and ill-prepared for meeting her own needs while simultaneously being there for Ron. We were very young and adulthood came on quickly with challenges we had never anticipated. Ron's boss and mentor died suddenly and Ron's radio world changed dramatically. He took a new job in Seattle, Washington, which required selling a home, finding a new one, and moving the family to a new community where we knew no one. This was all happening at the same time our second son was coming into the world. We clung to each other like shipwreck survivors in very rough seas. While this tested our relationship, it also strengthened it and helped us bond. It was during this first decade of our relationship that we began to realize that problems were challenges and opportunities to grow.

Our thirties were about self-realization and discovering who we really are. It was a time of personal growth as we began to face, discuss and attempt to resolve our childhood wounds, misperceptions and unexamined beliefs that we'd picked up from our families. It was the nineteen seventies, the time of the human potential movement, and we had encountered a Northern California group named More House. They not only pushed our limits, they challenged our reality. More House provided an enormous impetus to see the world in a way that was different from what we had been taught all of our lives. More House taught that we are responsible for all aspects of our life, that it is perfect, and that we are never victims of circumstances. It was the first time that we were introduced to the concept that we create our reality. During encounter groups we were put on the hot seat and given an opportunity to examine our lives. The difference between who and how we pretended to be and what we really felt was exposed. We began to share with each other the deeper truth of our feelings and desires. We were beginning to change, but we still hadn't taken the big step of claiming total responsibility. We now know that the Universe unfolds as it should one hundred percent of the time, but at that time we believed the Universe unfolds as it should…about sixty-two percent of the time.

We were each still following our life-long custom of blaming. We look back on this phase as the time when we learned spiritual fighting. We'd each throw spiritual concepts at the other in an attempt to make the other person wrong. However, in the midst of all of this, we knew that something had to give. In 1974 we made a decision to leave the life we had created and embark on a trip around the United States. We used to joke about how the cords between us had gotten so tangled that we didn't know what to do with the knotted ball of string that was our relationship. So, we decided to just throw the ball away, rather than our relationship, and start all over again. We dropped our history, our stories. We left the past in the past, moved into the present moment and began a grand adventure. That became our magical mystery tour, a six month motor home journey around the United States with our two sons. We found ourselves in a position of not knowing anyone as we traveled from town to town exploring totally new territory. Once again we clung to each other for dear life and found another opportunity to bond, this time not only with each other, but with our sons as well. Upon our return from this six month odyssey we picked up the pieces of the life that we had left behind. We discovered we couldn't do it alone. Denny began seeing a psychotherapist and before long convinced Ron that we needed a guide to help get us through our relationship issues.

Then came our forties. Denny's career path began to emerge. Now that the children were nearly grown, she returned to graduate school to pursue her dream of becoming a Marriage and Family Therapist. During this decade our sons left home and we adjusted to having an empty nest. We had to take a look at who we were now that the children were no longer the focus of our attention. Between our twenties and our forties life provided the necessary ingredients that allowed us to learn to function in a whole new way. We had gone from dependent, to independent, to interdependent. As newlyweds we had been very dependent on each other. After a decade of marriage and good psychotherapy we had learned that we were separate beings with our own life paths, challenges and successes. Once the boys moved out to establish their own lives, we were left to discover the meaning of interdependence. We learned to hold on to our individual selves and at the same time trust and share with each other. We learned that each of us could rely on the other. With this new way of being together, we were able to go back and resolve the unresolved issues that we had put aside. Ron experienced great success as a broadcaster. Denny established her psychotherapy practice. We enjoyed our individual successes and took pleasure in our partner's success.

With our fifties came more complex issues. It sort of snuck up on us, the fact that we had indeed achieved financial security, despite a number of poor investment decisions in our forties. Grandchildren also came along, and with them an opportunity to revisit parenting issues from a larger perspective. As with most grandparents, we were able to view the grandchildren with a more relaxed attitude, having been through it once before. For us, our fifties were a time of huge spiritual growth as our attention turned from survival, acquiring, and maintaining to something less tangible and more nourishing. Friends and peers began dying. Very suddenly our parents aged and died. We were inspired to begin putting the pieces of consciousness and spirituality that we had been accumulating throughout our relationship into a form that we could share with others. Thus was born *The New Perspective*, our awakening to a reality where consciousness comes first, where we are

Spirit having a human experience. This became the basis for our writing and teaching.

As we journey through our sixties, the issues continue to change. We find ourselves involved in retirement, which has provided an opportunity for ongoing reassessment of values and finding ways to share all that we've learned. We find ourselves as elders of our tribe. When we became elders we took on a new role. We define it as sharing our journey so it can act as a marker for those who follow.

Relationship Wreckers or Opportunities to Grow?

Included in the lifetime experience of relationship are such challenges as dealing with the birth of children, relating to in-laws, blending families and having step children, struggling through illnesses and financial problems, dealing with infidelity and/or sexual identity issues, and much more. Every life has its unique set of circumstances. There are two ways we can view these: either as relationship wreckers or opportunities to grow. If you approach each problem as an opportunity to grow you get closer to the heart of who you are and closer to the heart of your partner.

There doesn't have to be any such thing as a relationship wrecker. Ron's dad used to say, "It's not what happens to you in life...it's what you do with what happens to you that counts." From this perspective everything that happens has the potential for being a blessing, if we perceive it as such. Since we have not chosen to live solitary lives of meditation in a cave, but have elected to experience life in a community, holding jobs, maintaining households, raising children, being active members of society, we have created a set of life circumstances that allow for our enlightenment in a very public way. We're not living in a cave—we're in the world—and subsequently the universe gives us worldly opportunities to advance. It's up to us to recognize the blessing in each of these circumstances.

For example, sometimes relationships change form. You may not always remain husband and wife, but the relationship, which added something to your life, exists nonetheless. If you take time to figure out what has been added to your life you will become more conscious, more awake, more grateful for having had the experience, rather than being bitter because of the break-up. Appreciate the relationships of your life, even the ones that have come and gone. Learn to value and appreciate your ex-husband or ex-wife by seeing the gift they brought you while you were together. Recognize the lessons you learned from the relationship.

In terms of ending relationships, you really never end them. Once you've truly loved someone, even if things change and you say you don't love them anymore, the truth is that special person is always with you. His or her memory stays with you and is forever in your heart. This is true whether the separation results from disagreement, divorce, or death. That person lives in your heart. We don't forget people we care enough about to be seriously involved with, even for a short period of time. They never leave our consciousness.

It is our belief that during a relationship we imprint each other with our energy. Just being in proximity to one another we pick up each other's energy. We have an impact on each other. We affect the energy of the other. We can't forget people who are written on our energy field. Everyone who has made an energy imprint on you stays with you forever. For this reason it's important to pay attention to who you hang out with...who or what you allow to impact your energy field. Are you allowing fear and violence or love and harmony into your life?

CHAPTER THIRTEEN

Sexuality and Sensuality

In this book we are addressing relationships that are sexually intimate. Because sexual energy is just that—energy, it has a natural flow and is part of the gift of life. It's not intrinsically good or bad: by its nature it produces pleasure. Unfortunately, many of us were taught to be frightened of anything that feels that good and we were taught to believe a price must be paid for such ecstasy. The prohibition against sexual pleasure is an invisible belief that exists within many of us. We may not know exactly how we came to believe sexuality is bad, but we usually acquire our sexual guilt by the time we reach puberty. Negative beliefs about sexuality have taken different forms with each generation, but they are pervasive. These cultural beliefs make it difficult to view sexuality and sensuality from a new perspective.

Denny's experience as a therapist with today's young people has enabled her to see a current generation that tends to dismiss the significance of sexual encounters. It's not uncommon for them to say that sex is "no big deal." Oral sex isn't even considered a sex act. In trivializing their sexual activity, today's young people miss the spiritual significance of this profound act of intimacy. Today's teen-age girls often use their sexuality as a way to gain power over the males in their lives. Low cut jeans, the thong, and the Brazilian bikini wax become tools for seduction and the deep inner bonds that can be forged in the sharing of sexual energy are lost. Young men also trivialize sexual encounters. "Hooking up" with the opposite sex becomes a sport. Many young men don't think twice about having sex with young women who are too drunk to be making intelligent choices. Making sex meaningless is just another way of reacting to sexual guilt. It is easier to minimize the significance of sexuality than to deal honestly with the issues that naturally arise. Which generation will forge the way in demonstrating that shame and guilt are inappropriate reactions to human exploration and enjoyment of our bodies? Which generation will discover and validate the understanding that pleasure is sacred and need not be feared? The New Perspective recognizes that sexuality is wholesome and that sexuality is also potent. The challenge is to be responsible with and respectful of this powerful force.

Sexuality is more than part of the reproductive process. Yes, it can produce babies, but it's far more than that. Sexuality is another expression of Spirituality—and is, in fact, an expression of our Spiritual nature in its highest form. When the ego or personality self is put aside and we truly connect Spirit to Spirit in the act of making love, we experience our Oneness. The ego has found many uses for sexual energy. It is used to sell all kinds of products, from cosmetics to clothes to cars. It can also be used to enslave; that happens in the sex industry with pornography and prostitution. It also happens in ordinary relationships when sex is used as a form of control. It's not unusual to hear men complain that "she won't give it to me," or to hear women complain that their mate demands too much sex. Sexuality isn't something you give or take or "tear off a piece of." At its highest form it's a sharing experience. Sexuality allows two people to become truly vulnerable to each other and in that vulnerable, undefended, open place, move together in Divine union.

Marriage vs. Spiritual Partnership

We believe that sexual energy and spiritual energy are one and the same. In the old paradigm of marriage, sexuality was necessary for reproduction and propagation of the species. In the new paradigm of Spiritual partnership, while propagation is not the goal, sexuality is still desirable because it creates a high vibratory frequency which produces shared ecstasy. The sexual energy of attraction that brings couples together is the same energy of attraction that holds the universe together and is the very force of creation. An ancient Greek belief was that Eros, sexual passion and attraction, was in fact the primordial force in the universe, which caused not only atoms, but all things to come together. Sexual energy—the energy of Spirit—*is* the energy of creation. Issues of sexuality are recognized as important to the marriage relationship, and they are equally vital to every Spiritual partnership, whether it's male/female, male/male, or female/female. Some of the differences between Spiritual partnership and marriage lie in the way partnerships work out their agreements in the areas of sexuality, trust and respect.

It has been our experience that in Spiritual partnership couples talk about how they feel and what they want, as opposed to having rules imposed upon them. Partners in a Spiritual relationship may decide certain unconventional aspects of sexuality are okay and that they do not have an issue with something people in a conventional relationship might label as weird or unusual.

In her practice, Denny has encountered more than one gay couple that has no issue whatsoever with having other partners. They talk about it ahead of time and they know where they stand with one another. There are no secrets and thus, no feelings of betrayal. Few married couples seem able to deal with anything outside of a monogamous relationship. In another example, a married couple may not feel comfortable with oral sex. Spiritual partners may agree that oral sex is a natural enhancement to their lovemaking. Instead of having rules imposed in keeping with the tradition of marriage, in a Spiritual partnership everything is open to discussion and mutual agreement.

☙❧

If we were to teach our children the naturalness of their sexuality and take the onus off of it, we would give them a companion for life. Sexuality is as much a part of us as breathing and yet we have attached so many moral judgments and fear-based beliefs to it that its natural energy flow is blocked. Did you celebrate when your child discovered his or her genitals for the first time? If not, why not?

Did your parents celebrate your self-discovery? What impact did their reaction have on you?

◎◎

In this culture's preoccupation with sex, we wind up putting so much attention and emphasis on genital contact that we miss out on the subtle opportunities to explore sensuality. Sensuality, unlike sexuality, encourages focus on each of our senses—not just our body parts. Attention to our five senses, hearing, tasting, touching, seeing, and smelling, makes us aware of the deep pleasure that being human provides. It is our belief that we also possess a sixth sense: imagination. This sixth sense is the most potent of them all. Focusing on each of the senses magnifies the sensual experience. As we pointed out in our first book, *The New Perspective: Ten Tools for Self-Transformation*, what you put your attention on expands. Time spent attending to each of the senses expands our ordinary awareness and moves us into states of expanded consciousness. The art of stimulating sexual body parts, coupled with sensual awareness, fueled by imagination, creates divine ecstasy.

Sacred Time

Couples need sacred time. Couples need a time of the week they can count on that is just for them and they do nothing else. There is no agenda. They don't tend to children or talk about work issues or answer ringing phones. Those bases all need to be covered so the couple can put full, undivided attention on each other. This sacred time is not the time to talk about finances, social obligations, work or family problems. It is a special time to be together, a "time-out" from day-to-day concerns. Sacred time could be lunch together or an evening dinner date or time alone in the bedroom after the children are asleep. The important thing is to be alone together on a regular basis so the two of you can count on having time that is dedicated exclusively to the relationship. The relationship needs to be nurtured.

We're suggesting you arrange sacred time together, not just date night or time for sex. We're proposing that in this sacred time you focus on enjoying the present moment with your partner. Be aware of each of your senses. Take time to truly enjoy the aroma and taste of your food while you're dining. Spend a moment truly looking at each other and the beauty that surrounds you. Listen to each other with your hearts open. Hold hands. Not all touch needs to be sexual. Make this a time to enjoy the pleasures available through all of your senses. That's what you have them for. Activate the imagination. Remember to dream together. These small details create a huge benefit in the development of an intimate relationship. Time spent sharing pleasure in this simple way is very satisfying. When you take time to do this with your partner, you will both find the experience deeply rewarding. If time and circumstance are appropriate, this may become the perfect prelude to sexual intimacy. Women need to feel close to have sex. Men need to have sex in order to feel close. Men and women need to understand this difference and learn to work with it so that everyone's needs get met in the relationship.

Three Sensuality Exercises

Not everyone reading this book will be able to complete all three of the following exercises. That's okay. You may choose to do whatever portion is comfortable for you.

Exercise Number One is designed to be done with a partner. Once you've taken time to experience sacred space as a couple, consider doing the following exercise. This sensate focus exercise can be used between you and your partner to open the lines of communication on the subject of pleasure. It also provides an opportunity to connect, through touch, in a way that is safe and sensual without producing anxiety. Plan to take a comfortable amount of time for this exercise. For some the comfort zone may be ten minutes; for others it may be twenty minutes or longer. This is meant to be a pleasurable, not a tedious experience. Decide who will be the Receiver. It is our experience that women go first when it's pleasurable; men go first when it's dangerous.

What to do: Prepare your space. You might want to dim the lights, put on soft music, and light candles. The Receiver undresses and lays face down. For the Giver, clothing is optional. The Giver begins a process of touch on the neck and shoulders that will eventually explore the whole body. The first time you do this, there is to be no genital contact because sexuality is not the goal. Learning what pleasures your partner is the goal. The touch should be a "taking touch." This means the Giver is actually taking pleasure in feeling the body of the Receiver. The best lovers take true pleasure in giving pleasure. For this reason, there is nothing for the Receiver to do. Throughout this portion of the exercise the Receiver's only job is to receive and to enjoy. We suggest that the Receiver, with eyes closed, go within and follow the Giver's touch from an inner place. This "taking touch" can be done with or without massage oil, depending on the preference of the Receiver. The Giver begins by asking the Receiver a series of questions that will help the Giver learn what kind of touch the Receiver prefers. While touching the Receiver's body, the Giver asks questions that only need to be answered yes or no. "Would you like me to touch softer? Would you like me to move slower? Do you prefer long strokes? Would you like more touching on this part of your body?"

The Giver needs to enjoy feeling the skin of the Receiver as if stroking velvet or satin. The Giver notices the breathing pace of the Receiver and synchronizes by breathing at the same pace. As this occurs, the two of you will begin to align your energy, blending in harmony as one. The Giver can practice feeling the subtle energy shifts in the Receiver as the exercise unfolds. Remember to explore frequently neglected parts of the body that are yearning to be touched. Touch the skin in the areas between the fingers and toes of your partner. Don't forget knees and elbows and underarms. Feet also ache to be pleasured. Givers need to continue checking with their Receivers to make sure that their touch continues to be pleasurable.

When the back of the body has been thoroughly explored, ask the Receiver to roll over and continue with your "taking touch," avoiding the genitals. Here is your opportunity to explore your partner's eyelids, ears, and lips in a gentle, caring manner. Remember to continue checking with the Receiver to make sure your touch is still pleasing, with the right speed and pressure. When the exercise is complete, and all appropriate parts of the body have been pleasured, embrace the Receiver with a full body hug. Both you and your partner may now look deeply into each other's eyes and give thanks for the pleasure of sharing this experience.

This concludes the first half of this experience. Now, or at a future time, repeat the exercise...changing roles. The Giver becomes the Receiver and the Receiver becomes the Giver. Learning to give and receive in equal measure creates a whole and complete relationship.

The Visiting Dignitary

Exercise Number Two does not require a partner. Before you can communicate to your partner your preferences for genital touching, you must be absolutely clear on what feels good—what turns you on. The following exercise should be done alone, taking as long as you desire to fully explore and excite your Inner Being. We first learned this exercise from More House in the nineteen sixties. They called it "Preparing for the Visiting Dignitary," and that's exactly how it should be approached. You are about to have an encounter with the most sacred and important person of your life. Prepare the room in advance. Make sure everything has been picked up and put away and the room is uncluttered and fit to receive your special visitor. Be sure the temperature is comfortable and the lighting is inviting. If you enjoy candles, light them. Consider adding your favorite music to the environment. Since touch is an important part of this experience, decide whether or not you prefer lotion or oil. If so, make sure it's available. We recommend using

Astroglide or K-Y jelly on your genitals. It's also a good idea to have a towel handy. And don't forget to include your favorite fragrance. If a favorite food excites the taste buds, provide it. Chocolate or wine can be very appropriate.

Once the room is prepared, the visiting dignitary arrives. It is you. Take a moment to enjoy the beauty of your surroundings. Make yourself comfortable. Remove your clothes and look at your body in a full length mirror. At first it may be difficult for you to enjoy looking at your body. In this culture we have been conditioned to dislike and judge parts of our bodies. As you do this part of the exercise your inner critic may begin chattering in your head, telling you what's wrong with your appearance, but the inner critic can be overcome. Stay with the process until you find one thing about your body that you like. Focus there. As you do, use your imagination and pretend that you're seeing your body for the very first time. Take away all preconceived notions and judgment and allow for appreciation and gratitude to replace the harshness of the inner critic. This body has served you well. It has carried you through all of your life experiences, allowing you to perceive the world around you. Bodies are like babies: they need to be loved. They need to be touched gently and lovingly. They need to be talked to softly and sensitively. They need to be honored. Don't feel discouraged if this is difficult for you. You may need to repeat this portion of the exercise a number of times until you become comfortable thinking of your body from this new perspective.

Since bodies like to be touched, that is the next step in the process. We recommend that you begin by touching your body in the same manner as in the previous exercise.

Begin away from the genitals and experiment until you find the perfect pressure, speed, and rhythm for you. Allow your pleasuring touch to journey wherever it's drawn, which will eventually be to your genitals. Don't forget to linger at the inner thighs and around the stomach using a soft touch and a circular motion. Then move on to the breasts, for both male and female explorers. We suggest you continue to experiment with a circular motion, beginning with large circles, coming in at your perfect pace to smaller and smaller circles until the nipple has been reached. Notice what touch triggers the sexual energy in you. In the future you're going to want to be able to communicate or describe this perfect touch to your partner. The goal is not orgasm: the goal is to become conscious of the process that builds the most sexual excitement leading to orgasm. Do this deliberately and with awareness.

Once you have experienced the perfect level of excitement with the breasts, proceed to the genitals. Your assignment here is to find your personal place of ultimate pleasure. Don't be in a hurry. Take lots of time. Once you've found your pleasure point, linger. Most women will find this ideal spot either to the left or right of the clitoris. The clitoris itself may be too sensitive to touch directly. See what works best for you. For men, the ultimate sensitivity is usually on the crown of the penis, but again explore the penis thoroughly to discover your personal preference. After you've found your personal pleasure point, slow down. Tease the sexual energy. Allow it to build up and just before the point of release, back off. Then build up again, and back off. See how many times you can take yourself up the ladder of sexual ecstasy before you reach the peak.

Once orgasm is achieved see what other pleasure may be available to you. Perhaps a firm touch on your genitals and other body parts may help ground you back into your body. This too can be a deeply pleasurable experience.

Sharing

Now that you've completed this solo exercise, it's time to share your discoveries with your partner. As before, you'll each have the opportunity to give and receive. For *Exercise Number Three*, add genital touching to *Exercise Number One*, while telling the Giver what pleasures you. It is very important for the Giver to listen sensitively to the Receiver as he or she shares their recently discovered personal preferences. It is at this point that you must follow their directions for sexual ecstasy. Don't let your ego get in the way. Don't hold on to the false notion that you know exactly what your partner likes. Don't complain that your partner should have told you sooner. You will learn something new about how your partner likes to be touched. It may surprise you. Be grateful that this intimate information is being shared, perhaps for the first time. You both now have the words, the technique, and your own personal experience to allow you to share with your partner your most intimate pleasure points.

CHAPTER FOURTEEN

The Joy Is in the Loving

If we have learned nothing else in more than 45 years together, we have learned that we did not come together in this relationship by accident. As individual creators of our personal realities we recognize that we have co-created this relationship to help each other have transformative experiences. We were drawn to each other by forces far greater than our individual personalities. We were swept up from distances hundreds of miles apart to be in the same place at the same time to complete a contract forged by our Higher Selves before we were born. When we first came together in 1959 at College of the Pacific in Stockton, California, we sensed on some level that we had something to give each other. And so, Love worked its magic. Ron found Denny attractive. Denny found Ron attractive. Her dad had been in radio. How could she not be attracted to a teenage disc jockey? Ron had been catered to and pampered for the first 18 years of his life. How could he not be attracted to a kind and beautiful young woman willing to love and care for him? And so, Spirit began orchestrating the unfolding of the relationship that would become "The Ron and Denny."

As we look back 45 years later, using the *Rearview Mirror Technique* that we describe in our first book, we can see the absolute perfection of Life's Divine Plan. We can see that our Higher Selves created just the right teachers who would help us learn our life lessons. We have fit each other perfectly, every step of the way. And the times that were the most perfect were the times we argued or tussled. The times we found ourselves struggling or in disharmony were the times we grew the most. When we were willing to be conscious and use the disharmony as a signal that something had come up that we needed to examine, we expanded and became aware of different aspects of ourselves.

As we pointed out earlier in this book, we've discovered we each have a unique, long-standing default position that has driven and challenged our relationship. Before becoming more conscious, Denny instinctively believed everything was "her fault." Ron defaulted to a belief that it was never "his fault." He always looked outside himself for the source of the problem. These two distinct default styles made us perfect partners and teachers for each other. We fit together like hand in glove: Ron looking to blame, Denny eager to take the blame. We suspect this "fault/no fault" dynamic may be a common one among couples. It may or may not apply to you and your partner. If this is not your life theme, we encourage you to use our *Rearview Mirror Technique* to see if you can discover your default positions.

The gift of our relationship has come from hanging in there, going through the disagreements, looking for the blessing in each situation—no matter how uncomfortable the experience. We've been able to do this because we have an absolute conviction that we create our reality, without exception. The universe unfolds as it should one hundred percent of the time, whether we can see it at the moment or not. Therefore, everything we experience is a blessing created *by us, for us*—even though it may not be apparent in the midst of our pain.

When we recognize that we have become blinded to the blessings inherent in our disagreements there is a tool we use that works one hundred percent of the time. That tool is forgiveness. Dropping the story of our grievance and forgiving the perpetrator takes us back to neutral ground. When we forgive the other, we no longer have to hold on to the pain of our alleged victimization. Forgiveness is a gift we give to ourselves. The kind of forgiveness we're talking about is found in the book *Radical Forgiveness,* by Colin Tipping. We direct you to his web site: www.radicalforgiveness.com.

This is not the traditional forgiveness that makes you a martyr. It's not done for the purpose of making you "a better person" who is letting someone off the hook. It is a radical forgiveness that recognizes that whether you can see it or not, the other person played his or her role perfectly in the drama of your life. It is forgiveness that recognizes there is nothing to forgive.

@/@

To feel loved, love. Become conscious that love is a feeling and that all feelings are self-generated. We tend to believe that love is something we receive from someone else, so we go around looking to be loved as if it were something someone could give us. But love is not something someone can pour into us: it is a feeling. It happens inside us and it comes from us. No one can give it; we have to generate it on our own.

When you are looking to receive, you're at the mercy of outside forces. When you're giving, you're in charge and you're allowing love's energy to move through you. So the joy is always in the loving. In addition to giving love and appreciation to others, you can also give it to yourself. When you do, you honor the Self's connection to the Divine.

APPENDIX

During our years together our relationship has evolved. What began as a traditional marriage has grown into a Spiritual Partnership. The following ceremony was created by Denny, who is also a Universal Life Church minister, for couples who choose to walk this new path. We offer these words to any of you who wish to redefine your relationship.

Ceremony for a Spiritual Partnership

Friends of the heart, companions of the Soul: we gather to witness the coming together of this couple in Spiritual Partnership—a union based in unconditional love...a partnership made on earth, embodying the essence of the Divine.

This couple has chosen to journey a new path...to establish a Spiritual Partnership. A union existing in this now moment, it possesses ever-awakening consciousness and is guided by the heart.

Recognizing their strength, they are open to each other. Honoring each other's ideals, they come together in loving support on their journey to the Oneness.

Spiritual Partners use their relationship to awaken.
Each struggle is an opportunity to grow. Each problem faced is a gift in raising consciousness.

This relationship honors the sovereignty of the other as a separate being and celebrates the reality of our Oneness.

As friends and companions, you can serve this couple now and in the future by holding this relationship in the most positive of perspectives...ever encouraging their love for each other... and reminding them in times of trouble that they are indeed partners on the same path.

In recognizing their commitment to each other, you can affirm your own commitment to Spiritual growth, honoring each of your relationships as a sacred opportunity to experience the Divine.

Acknowledgments

The cover of this book is the delicious work of Sedona artist Trea Christopher Grey, with graphic design by Kimall Christensen, www.worldsofgoodfortune.com.

Book editing and invaluable assistance in every phase of this endeavor came from Dr. Leda Ciraolo, The Written Word, Oakland, California, ledaciraolo@sbcglobal.net.

This book could not have been written without the many contributions to our lives made by a number of wonderful people. We are grateful to all those friends of the heart and companions of the soul who have supported us on our journey.

We also express our deep appreciation to Victor Baranco, Dr. Anna Harelson, Darryl Anka and Bashar, and *A Course in Miracles* for all they taught us. We have special gratitude to Sai Baba for his eternal love.

For information on workshops and events we invite you to visit our web site: www.thenewperspective.com.

For additional copies of this book:
Order on line at: www.trafford.com/06-0073.html

Other Trafford books by Ron and Denny Reynolds
The New Perspective: Ten Tools for Self-Transformation
Order on-line at: www.trafford.com/04-2593.html

Or contact:
Trafford Publishing
Suite 6E, 2333 Government St.
Victoria, BC, Canada V8T4P4
Phone 250-383-6864
Toll free 1-888-232-4444 (Canada and US only)

CPSIA information can be obtained
at www.ICGtesting.com
Printed in the USA
FFHW021948260719
53898405-59616FF